CW01171500

ERRATA

PAGE 89. Aneometer should be Anemometer.

PAGE 59, 61 and 141. In the names of octaves lined, after numerals, should be line.

A Treatise on the Construction Repairing and Tuning of the
Organ

Including also the Reed Organ, the
Orchestrelle and the Piano-Player

❋

With numerous illustrations

❋

By

Oliver C. Faust

Principal of the Tuning Department
New England Conservatory of Music
Boston ======= Massachusetts

Printed for the
Author

MB

Copyright © 2006 Merchant Books

ISBN 1-933998-31-8

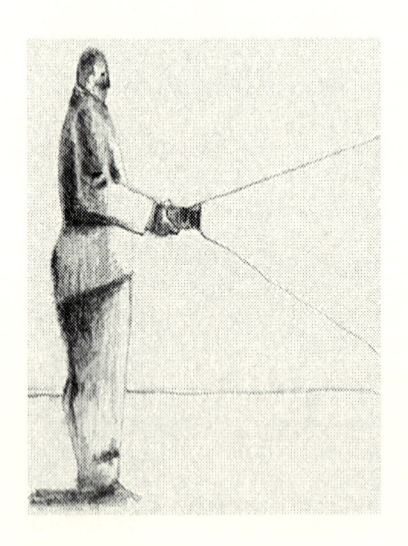

PREFACE

This little hand-book is the outgrowth of a teaching experience extending over several years. It has been compiled to meet a want as yet unfilled; for no book has come to my attention that treats, within a brief compass, of the construction of the organ with any definiteness. The endeavor has been to describe the construction of the different styles of actions used in the pipe organ with a minuteness that will enable the student to understand the construction and operation of each part of this complex instrument. To this has been added in brief outline a description of the construction of the reed organ, piano-player, and orchestrellé.

A Practical Treatise on the History, Construction, Repairing, and Tuning of the Organ

The word organ in its early use, signified an instrument of any kind, but was applied more particularly to musical instruments. It is probable that the first organ building dates back to the syrinx, or pipes of prehistoric Pan, which were in use among a number of primitive peoples. This instrument consisted of a number of pipes or reeds arranged in a row, with respect to the succession of their tones; thus forming a mouth organ composed of from seven to eleven hollow reeds tied together or joined with wax, and placed on a level in order that the mouth could easily pass from one pipe to the next. These pipes were sounded by the admission of wind. Playing on them was no doubt tiresome, as supplying them with wind was necessarily accompanied by a movement, from side to side, of the head of the performer. Later this arrangement of the pipes or reeds had attached to it a wind-chest.

First Use of the Wind-chest

For centuries endeavors were made to make easier the operation of the pipes. One of the first of the resulting improvements was the invention of a wooden box, in the top of which holes were bored to receive the feet of the pipes which were arranged according to size. From this hollow box no doubt developed the modern wind-chest. This latter was provided with wind, by blowing into a small tube which led into the chest.

In a chest of this style there was nothing to prevent all the pipes speaking at the same time, and the only way to avoid this disagreeable feature, was to close with the fingers the ends of the pipes that were to remain silent. As the pipes increased in number it was impossible to control them in this manner; thus it became necessary to furnish each pipe with a valve, or piston, which controlled the admission of wind to it. See figure 1, page 7.

As the organ developed, and the number of pipes increased, the wind-chest was proportionately enlarged. This addition in chest and pipes required a greater supply of wind, and as it was impossible for human lungs to meet this demand, it was necessary to devise some form of bellows, that would adequately supply the pipes with moving air. A bellows was invented similar to that used in the ordinary household; it was nevertheless efficient for the needs of that time. See figure 2, page 7.

Valves, and How They Were Connected

In this simple organ, the valves were connected with cords, which were probably the origin of the modern "pull-down." But the

Fig. 1

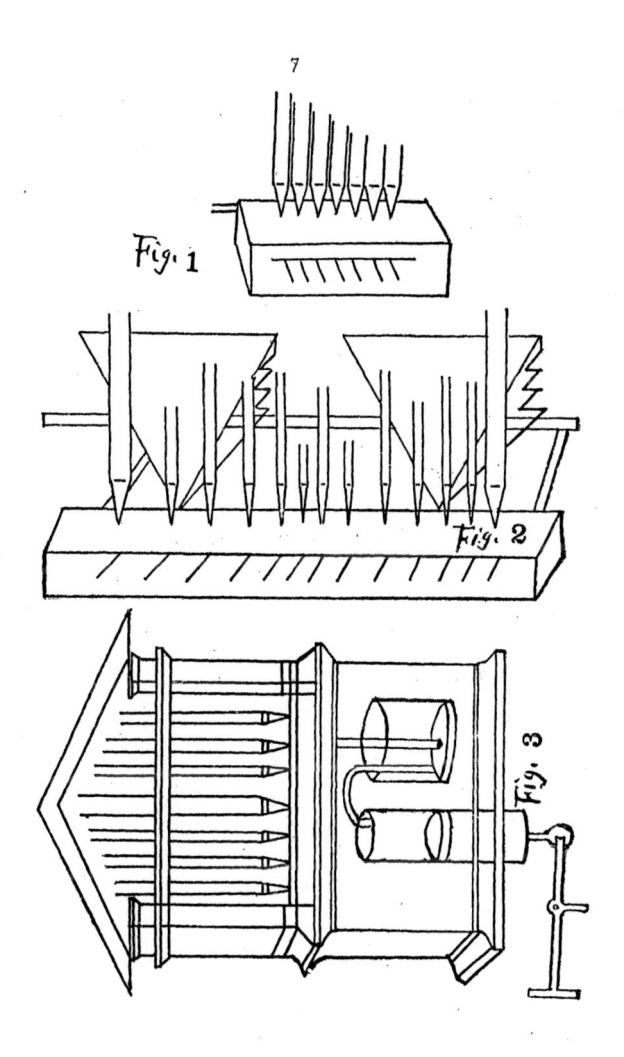

Fig. 2

Fig. 3

bellows were found to be inadequate. By referring to the diagram of this organ, figure 2, page 7, it will be seen that the means of supplying the chest with wind was very unsatisfactory, as the bellows, which corresponded to the present "feeders," did not furnish a steady wind pressure.

Bellows, and How They Were Fastened

Pressure uneven. Both bellows were fastened to the same pump rod, and moved in the same direction; accordingly when they returned to refill, they caused an uneven pressure of the air; and as a result of this unevenness in wind pressure, the tone of the organ would be correspondingly unsteady.

Hydraulic or Water-Organ

The date of the invention of this organ is unknown, but in all probability it was before the birth of Christ. The deficiency in wind pressure made it necessary to seek other means of supplying the organs with wind. This was accomplished by using the hydraulic or water-organ, in which water was used to force the air to the pipes, much after the manner of the action of the weight placed on the bellows of to-day.

Athenæus, who flourished in the third century, has left us probably the most ancient and authentic account extant of the hydraulic organ. He tells us that it was invented in the time of the third Ptolemy Euergetes by the barber Ctesibius, a native of Alexandria (B. C. 200); or rather it was improved by him, for Plato furnished the first idea of the hydraulic-organ, by inventing a night clock which was a clepsydra, or water-clock, that played upon flutes the hours of the night at a time when they could not be seen on the index.

The following is a description of the hydraulic-organ. The air was forced from a cylinder into a tank containing water, and from there into the pipes. The cylinder had a close-fitting piston, controlled by a rod connected with a lever. Each stroke of the piston forced the air out of the cylinder through a tube into the tank. The piston in this cylinder worked very much on the same plan as that of the common bicycle pump.

After being forced into the tank the air was compressed by lifting a disc which fitted so closely to the inside of the tank that it formed a water tight joint. The upper portion of this tank received a sufficient quantity of water, to compress the air to the desired bulk measured in inches.

As will be seen by referring to figure 3, page 7, the water in the tank, as before remarked, served the same purpose as the weight placed on the top of the bellows of the modern organ. In the center of the disc in the tank, was placed a tube or conductor, to lead the wind to the pipes.

From the first century water organs were used to accompany the performers in the Roman theaters. It is thought that the later invention of a bellows, dates from the time of Emperor Julian, in the fourth century. Yet this great improvement in furnishing wind, was not used extensively until the end of the ninth century, at which time Germany became the center of organ building.

The organ was first used for religious worship as early as the middle of the fifth century. A Spanish Bishop, Julianus, writes that it was then in common use in the churches of Spain. Mention is made of an organ being used in the Church of the Nuns at Grado about the year 580; and a description of it is as follows: Length of organ 2 feet, width 6 inches, number of pipes 30, two to each note. The admission of wind to the pipes was controlled by fifteen slides. The mode of operation of the slides is probably not known.

The art of organ building was known in England in the beginning of the eighth century. Aldhelm, who died A. D. 709, tells us that the Anglo-Saxons decorated the show pipes with gilding.

In the middle of the eighth century, an organ was presented by the Byzantine Emperor Constantine to the Church of St. Corneille at Compiegne, France, in which pipes made of lead were used. St. Dunstan's organ had pipes which were made of brass. St. Dunstan died A. D. 988.

The Early Construction of Large Organs

At the close of the ninth century, large organs were built for some of the churches of Rome, in which thirty bellows were employed to furnish wind. The necessity for so many bellows, was owing to their imperfect construction. Placing weight on the bellows had not yet been thought of, so that the wind pressure depended entirely on the strength of the men operating them. Under such conditions it was impossible to have the organ in tune, as the pressure of wind was too uneven.

In the ninth century English builders constructed organs with pipes of copper fixed in gilt frames. An interesting account is given by the monk Wulston of a monster organ, built about the close of the tenth century for the Winchester Cathedral. This organ had twelve pairs of bellows which were worked by seventy strong men. Its pipes numbered four hundred. The compass did not exceed ten notes, forty pipes to each note, and all sounded at the same time. The pipes were made to sound by levers or rods, as the keyboard had not yet been invented. The separation of the wind in the chest by sliders was not known at that time. Wulston died A. D. 963.

Compass of the Keyboard

In these ancient organs the player could not reach the compass of an octave, even with outstretched arms. In playing, the keys were struck hard blows with the fist, instead of being pushed down by the pressure of the fingers. The organist was often called a Pulsator.

In some cases the keys were five and a half inches broad, and forty-five inches long; the dip being proportionately deep. They numbered from nine to eleven, and were shaped very much like a violin. It is probable that these instruments shrieked in a loud, harsh manner.

At this epoch in the growth of the organ, harmony was unknown. The plain chant of that day did not require a larger compass, than that mentioned, although of course nothing but a choral melody for one voice could be played on an organ of this style.

Gradually, however, the width of the keys was decreased until the fifth equalled the present octave. In the twelfth century the number of keys was increased, and about that time, two or three pipes were added to each key, tuned to the fifth, octave, or major third. It seems that this was the beginning of the mixture.

Earliest Use of Semitones

The earliest account of the use of semitones in the organ dates from the fourteenth century. The improvements then made increased the range of the organ to nearly three octaves.

The Addition of Pedals

At about the same time pedals were added by a German musician named Bernhard. These various improvements were due for the most part to the Germans, and consequently they acquired an extensive reputation as organ builders.

Ancient Organs With Two Keyboards

In the fourteenth century large churches often had two organs, a large and a small one. The large organ had two keyboards, the upper one being used for the treble, and the lower one for the bass. This arrangement of the organ no doubt suggested the need of a coupler, the invention of which soon followed.

The Keyboard Improved

In this century the keyboard was improved. As we have mentioned, up to this time the keys had been large, the action heavy, and the dip deep, making it necessary in playing to strike them with the fist; and the range of the keyboard had been very small.

The fifteenth century organs in cathedrals had keyboards the span of whose octave was equal in width to nine notes of the present keyboard. The action, moreover, was still very heavy and clumsy.

Positive Organ

The Positive Organ when being played was placed upon a table, and the pumper standing behind furnished wind with a pair of small hand bellows. The keyboard had a sufficient compass to allow the organist to play with both hands. It is probable that the positive organ was the ancestor of the choir organ.

Before the organ had more than one keyboard, the term "pair of organs" was used; which doubtlessly meant an organ with more than one pipe.

The Addition of Reed Pipes

In the sixteenth century reed pipes were added, and the compass was increased to four octaves. In this same century a bellows with one fold was invented, and this form of bellows is still used in old organs, especially those of Europe.

The Wholesale Destruction of Organs in England

During the time of the great rebellion in England, on January 4th and May 9th., 1644, an ordinance was passed in the House of Lords, abolishing superstitious monuments in all cathedrals, parish churches and chapels. This included the destruction of organs. It read as follows: "The Lords and Commons in Parliament, the better to accomplish the blessed reformation so happily begun, and to remove all offenses and things illegal in the worship of God, do ordain that all representations of the Trinity or any angel, etc., etc., in and about any cathedral, collegiate or parish churches and chapels, shall be taken away, defaced and utterly demolished, and that all organs and the frames and cases wherein they stand in all churches and chapels aforesaid shall be taken away and utterly defaced and none other hereafter set up in their places." By the enforcing of this ordinance, the churches were stripped of their organs and ornaments. A number of the instruments were sold to private persons who preserved them, but many were totally, and others partially destroyed. The clergy in order to save some of the instruments, took them away.

The sequences of these acts are in keeping with their destructiveness. The soldiers were quartered in the Abbey Church, where they broke down the altar and burnt it where it stood. "They destroyed the organs and pawned the pipes at several ale houses for pots of ale. They put on some of the singing men's surplices and in contempt of that canonical habit, ran up and down the church. He that wore the surplice was the hare, the rest were the hounds." They went up and down the streets at Exeter with two or three hundred pipes they had taken from the organs they had destroyed, and in scornful manner sounding the pipes when meeting with some of the choristers of the church and scoffingly saying: "Boys, we have spoyled your trade; you must goe and sing hot pudding pyes." While the soldiers were at the Nunnery at Little Gidding in Huntingdonshire, the house and church were both ransacked. They broke the organ in pieces, using the material for a fire over which they roasted and made merry on a number of Mr. Ferrer's sheep, which they had killed within his grounds.

During the period of sixteen years, between the date of the ordinance and the Restoration, organ builders were compelled to

Fig. 4.

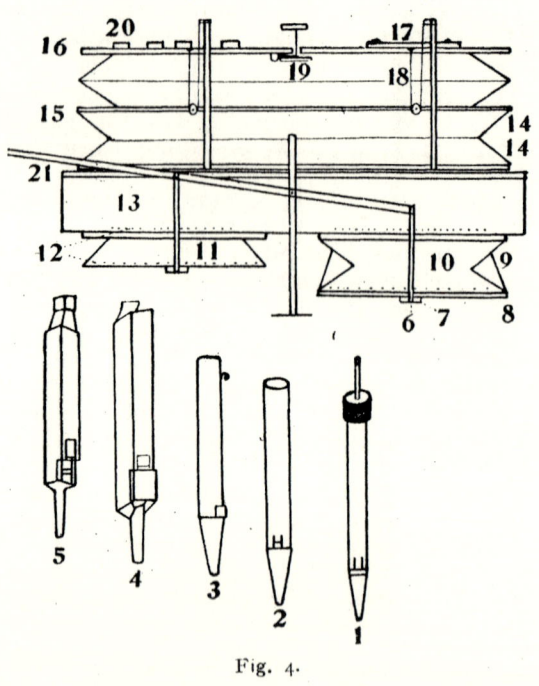

work as carpenters and joiners. At the expiration of this interval a sufficient number of workmen for the immediate supply of organs not being available, it became necessary to send for foreign builders to settle in England. With the renewed interest in organ building there were developed two celebrated workmen, Smith and Harris.

The First Organ Building in America

It was three quarters of a century after this revival of organ building in England that, in 1737, the first organ was built in America by Mathias Zimmerman, of Philadelphia. In 1745, Edward Bromfield built an organ in Boston; and in 1752 Thomas Johnson built an organ for Christ Church, in that city.

The Modern Pneumatic or Wind Organ

Ancient organs, as has already been stated, were deficient in the pressure of wind, which was very uneven. This was overcome to some extent in the hydraulic organ, that was in such high favor, and which no doubt owed its fame to the contrivance by which water was used so as to overcome the unevenness of pressure. (See figure 3, page 7.)

The organ of to-day is called the pneumatic or wind organ, and we shall now describe its construction in such detail as to make its action clear.

The Bellows and its Use

The use of the bellows is to collect, compress, and force atmospheric air through the various wind trunks and chests, to the pipes. (See figure 4, page 16.) The bellows used in church organs are of two kinds, horizontal and diagonal. The horizontal bellows are the commonly adopted form, and formerly they were made very much like the common household bellows. The horizontal bellows maintains its surface on a level in all stages of its movements; thus it is able to accumulate a far larger quantity of wind than the diagonal bellows which is wedge shaped and is operated at only one end, which reduces the supply of wind one-half.

Inventor of the Bellows

It is supposed that Samuel Green, an Englishman was the inventor of the horizontal bellows, as he provided several organs with them in 1787 and 1788.

The Middle Board

The top board forms the top or roof to the bellows. The middle board is placed between the bellows and the feeders, and thus serves the double purpose of bottom to the bellows and roof to the feeders. The middle board being the fixture of these three boards, supports the weight of the bellows, while below hang the feeders.

The middle board is a little larger than the top board, as on it rests the trunk band, which is made of strong material. The bottom board forms the bottom of the feeders.

Middle and Bottom Board Valves

The valves on the middle and bottom boards, are made of sheep-skin and are usually hinged at both ends. The openings in the bottom board are called suckers; through these the air enters the feeders.

Middle Board Panels

Sometimes the middle board is furnished with panels, in order to permit easy access to the valves on the bottom board when they need repairing.

Feeders, Weight, and Wind-gauge

The feeders force the air up, and the weight placed on the bellows presses the latter down. In weighting a bellows it is not wise to use stones, as in damp weather they absorb moisture and increase in weight, and in dry weather lose weight; thus the organ will change in tone and tune. The wind is measured by the use of the wind gauge. (Figure 5, page 20, numbers 4-5.) The surface weight required to produce the compressed organ air, such as would give an inch wind on a bellows, is about three pounds and five and one third ounces per superficial foot on the top board. Therefore to produce a three inch wind, the average amount of weight will be ten pounds per superficial foot.

Inverted Ribs

In the bellows of to-day the inverted ribs are used, and these are so arranged that the upper ones hinge outwards and the lower

Fig. 5.

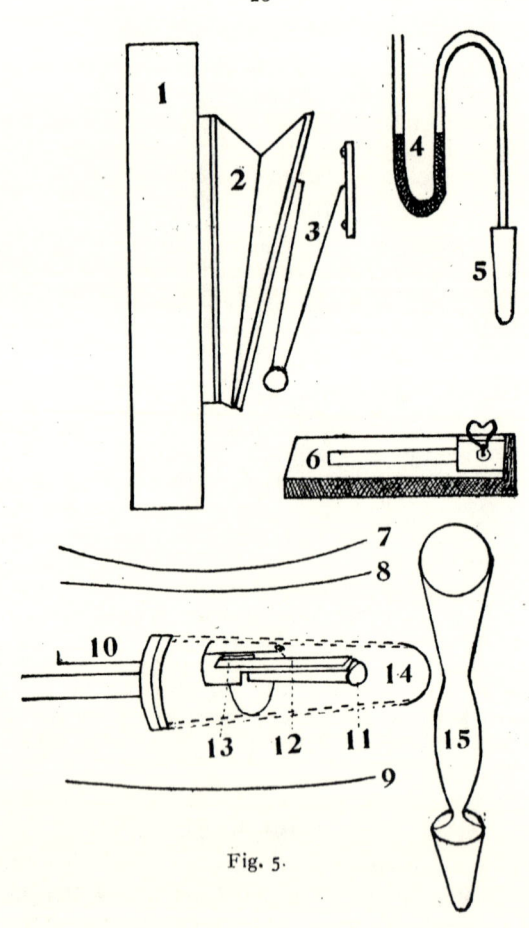

ones hinge inwards. The advantage of this arrangement, is that they produce an equal pressure of wind.

By use of these compensation folds the gain is from one-fourth to three-eighths of an inch. The folds ought never to reach an angle greater than forty-five degrees.

Middle Frame

The middle frame is simply a surrounding frame of wood to which is fastened the lower edge of the upper ribs, and the upper edge of the lower ribs.

The Wind Box

The wind box or well, is only used in some large organs. It is placed under the bottom board, or at one side of the bellows. The advantage of this arrangement is, that the wind can be taken from any point desired. It also gives more freedom to the air. Without using the wind box, the wind must be taken from the end of the bellows.

The Blowing of the Organ

On the bottom board there is attached a lug or hook, to which the levers of the bellows' handle are connected. So that by its stroke the bottom board is raised toward the middle board, which forces the atmospheric contents of the feeder through the openings in the middle board into the bellows; and this raises the top board.

The simplest means of obtaining an equal pressure of wind, is to have two feeders.

They can be either beneath or at one side of the bellows. The bottom board of the feeder is hinged at the center, or at one side of the middle board.

Blowing Action

The arrangement by which the feeders of the bellows are put in motion, is called the blowing action. There is a telltale or indicator, fastened to the bellows in such a manner as to aid the blow boy in keeping the desired supply of wind.

Square Feeder

In some organs the feeders are not diagonal and hinged at one side or end, but they are square and preserve a level state in all their movements; by which means they gain a great deal of power over the old wedge-shaped feeder, and are better able to supply air to the bellows. The gain of the square feeder is from one-third to one-half more than that of the diagonal arrangement, which is operated by use of the rocker action.

The Arrangement of the Ribs

The ribs of the bellows are first arranged in pairs; the edges of each pair are brought close together, after which there is a long narrow piece of sheep-skin glued along the entire length of the ribs. There is also a second piece attached to the other side. These pieces form the hinge which is called the middle joint. The openings at the ends, which are called gussets, are then closed with leather.

Detailed Description of the Horizontal Bellows.
(See Figure 4, page 16.)

6. *Pump-rod.* The lower end of the pump-rod is secured to the lug by an iron bolt, the upper end being placed in a mortise cut in the bellows' handle and secured by an iron pin or bolt.

7. *Lug.* The lug is a piece of wood projecting from the movable end of the feeder. It is fastened by screws to the bottom board of the feeder. The end of the lug receiving the pump-rod is fork-shaped.

8. *Bottom-Board.* One side of this board is hinged to the middle board; the other side is free to move up and down with the pump-rod.

9. *Folds or Ribs.* The folds are pieces of wood joined together by several pieces of strong webbing and sheep-skin. They are fastened to the middle and bottom boards with the same material.

10. *Feeder Ready for Action.* When a feeder is in the position shown in the drawing (Figure 4, page 16,) it is filled with air ready to be forced into the bellows.

11. *Feeder After Action.* Figure 4, page 16, shows the position of the feeder after the air has been forced into the bellows.

12. *Valve-holes.* The valve-holes are in the middle and bottom boards, and are covered with sheep-skin; but they are not as close together as represented in the diagram.

13. *Trunk-band.* The trunk-band is made of thick pieces of board; the wind-

trunks are fastened to it at the most convenient point.

14. *Ribs or Folds of Bellows.* The lower set of bellows' ribs hinge in, while the upper set hinge out; by placing the ribs in these opposed positions, they neutralize each other.

15. *Middle-frame.* To this frame are attached the lower edge of the upper ribs, and the upper edge of the lower ribs; thus the frame holds the ribs firmly in position.

16. *Top-board.* The top-board is usually made of pine boards, having a thickness of from one to two or more inches; this board being strongly made, the stability of the bellows is increased.

17. *Panel.* The panel is a board covering an opening left in the top-board large enough to allow an easy means of access into the interior of the bellows, to repair the valves when they become disarranged or destroyed by mice or rats.

18. *Counter-balance.* The counter-balance consists of strong cord, and small pulleys fastened to the middle-frame by a screw. One end of the cord is attached to the top-board; the other to a standard fastened to the trunk-band. The counter-balance keeps the ribs at an equal distance. It also prevents the top-board from swinging to and fro. Another form of counter-balance, not shown in the cut, consists of three flat pieces of iron or wood fixed, on a pivot, to the top-board, middle-frame and trunk-band; these pieces are mova-

ble at every joint. A bellows is usually furnished with four of the above counter-balances two at each side.

19. *Escape-valve.* When the bellows reaches a certain height, the escape-valve, which is fastened on the under side of the top board, comes in contact with a wooden pin, fastened in a stationary board, which is so placed that there are but four or five inches between it and the bellows. When the bellows is at its highest point the pin opens the valve, and allows the wind to escape when more is supplied than is needed. Thus the density of the organ wind is not increased beyond the required degree.

20. *Weights.* The weights are placed on the top-board for the purpose of forcing it down, thereby compressing the air.

Bars of iron or lead are better suited for this purpose than bricks or stones.

21. *Bellows-handle.* This is connected with the pump-rod and is used to put in motion the feeders.

Repairing Bellows and Feeders. In gluing leather on the bellows or feeders or on cracked wind-trunks or chests, rub the glued parts with a piece of cloth thoroughly wrung out in hot water. The heat will warm the parts so rubbed and cause the glue to enter the pores of the leather and wood, thereby insuring their adhesion. Also, by rubbing, press out and remove all surplus glue.

Pressure of Wind. Most organs are built to use a wind pressure of three to four inches.

At the present time there is a tendency to increase the pressure of some part of the organ to 8, 10, 15, or even 20-inch wind. The strength of the voice compared with that of the pipe organ is from 9 to 10 inches.

Concussion Bellows. We should naturally suppose after all these improvements in feeders and bellows, that the pressure of the wind would be steady. But if many of the large pipes were suddenly made to speak or to cease speaking, there would be an unsteadiness of tone, because of the fact that if a large supply of air is drawn suddenly from the wind-chest, the remaining air will expand by its own elasticity, and cause a pulsation. This defect is remedied by the introduction of the concussion bellows or reservoir which is attached with a spring to the side of a wind trunk for the purpose of forcing the movable board toward the trunk. (See Figure 5, Page 20, Numbers 1, 2, 3.)

The Purpose of Wind-Trunks

The wind has now been collected and compressed, as already stated, and is ready to be distributed among the different divisions or departments of the organ. The distribution is accomplished by the use of conductors, or wooden tubes, called wind trunks.

It is just as important to have a sufficient means for conveying the wind, as it is to supply it. Wind trunks vary in size, according to the distance of the sounding-board from the bellows, and the size of the organ, or number of stops it contains, whether they are on a large or small scale. They range in size from four to eighteen inches in width, from three to six inches in depth, and from two to fifteen feet in length. Wind trunks are seldom jointed at right angles, as a right angle checks the flow of air.

Prompt Speech of the Organ

If the bellows and sounding board are close together, the speech of the organ will be more prompt and clear than when they are far apart.

Wind-Chests and Sounding-Board
TRACKER ORGAN

The wind has now been conveyed from the bellows, through the trunks to the wind chests. A wind-chest is a long, broad and shallow wooden case or box. It is the same length as the sounding-board, to which it belongs, and is from one-half to two-thirds as broad; it is from eight to twelve inches deep. The wind in the chest is now ready for further use. The wind-chest serves as a second reservoir, so arranged as to receive a portion of the air accumulated in the bellows, and to distribute it to the various pipes, after the manner to be mentioned a little later.

The back of the chest is called the wind bar. It consists of heavy material, and is as long and deep as the chest which it supports. The weight of the pipes has a tendency to cause a sagging in the sounding-board, or top of the chest, on which it rests.

Front-board or Bung

The front-board or bung as it is called, is made movable, as the pallets or valves are liable to get out of order, and therefore should be easy of access.

Pull-down Wire

Directly under each pallet, a hole is drilled in the bottom of the wind-chest, through which the pull-down wire passes, to the point where it is connected with the key movement. These holes are made much larger than the pieces of wire, to prevent the sticking which dampness would cause.

To prevent the escape of wind on account of the extra size of these holes, there is a narrow plate of brass placed underneath the chest; through which plate holes are drilled just large enough to allow the pull-down to work freely. On the ends of the pull-downs there are loops, through which the hooks of the trackers are fastened.

Sounding-Board

For every key on the organ there is a small oblong groove. These grooves are divided by partitions into as many compartments or channels, as there are keys. If there are sixty-one keys on a manual, there will be the same number of grooves, and all pipes of a particular note of the key-board, are placed over this air passage. Sometimes the larger pipes need a greater supply of wind for the prompt speech of the pipes, and this necessitates a double groove.

Pallets or Valves

In the wind-chest, over these grooves, are placed the pallets, and in the movable end of these the pallet eye is fastened.

The pull-downs passing through the small holes in the bottom of the wind-chest, are attached to the pallets by means of hooks on the pull-downs, which are connected with the key movement. The valves are covered with soft leather, to make them fit closely and work quietly. The pallets taper by degrees, and by this tapering aid the valves, in pushing their way through the compressed air.

The valve is made a little larger than the width of the groove. The less the valve extends beyond the valve-hole on each side and end, the less space there will be to rest on the cushion for any foreign substance that might fall through the sounding-board.

Direction Pins

The valves are provided with two wires called direction pins, one on either side to guide them in their ascent and descent.

A Running of Air

Sometimes air will escape through a groove, and force its way up to a pipe, which will cause the pipe to produce a continuous low sound, that is technically called "ciphering." There are several reasons tor this.

First, a sounding-board bar may have become warped, or partially separated from the table, which allows a leakage of wind from one groove to the next. This is permanently remedied by removing the top of the wind-chest, in order to fill in and cover the defect. This leakage may be temporarily remedied by making a small hole in the groove through the cheek, which allows the air to escape. This is called bleeding, and is not a proper way to relieve the trouble.

Second, the upper-boards may be too loose. This can be remedied by tightening the upper-board screws a little.

Third, a bar may be unsound. This can be remedied by gluing a piece of sheep-skin over the crack. When a pipe is below, above, or at one side of the sounding-board, a metal tube, called a conveyance is made use of, to conduct the wind from the groove or groove-board to the pipe.

Sliders, Bearers, and Pipe Racks

The sliders are long, narrow, flat, movable slips of wood, lying over the series of holes in the table. They are pierced throughout with holes, which correspond with those in that part of the table on which they rest, and also with those in the upper-board. The sliders serve to admit or exclude wind from the pipes of a set where the stop is not drawn: they thus become the wind regulating features. On drawing a slider which is perforated with holes, exactly corresponding with those in the table over the grooves, and exactly under those in the upper-board, the three now agreeing, the air can pass up from any groove into which it may be admitted, into the pipes of the stop that is out.

The sliders are so arranged that they can be moved from right to left. In one end there is a hole that receives the end of the stop lever. This lever is used in moving the slider backwards and forwards. In the other end there is a second hole, through which passes a strong iron pin. This pin is fastened to the table, to prevent the slider from moving too far either way. If this motion were not prevented, the slider might shut off part of the wind. This would prevent the pipes from speaking with proper tone, and thus throw them out of tune. Sometimes there is a third hole in the slider which allows the composition pedal to act.

The bearers support the upper-boards which are screwed down on to them, and sustain the weight of the upper-boards and pipes, thus relieving the sliders, from all pressure, and insuring for them freedom of action.

The pipe-rack-boards or rack-boards, are placed in line with the sounding-board, with but four or five inches between the rack and upper-boards. They are held in position, by rack pillars placed at the corners and other convenient places. The rack-boards are furnished with holes cut exactly over those in the upper-boards. The foot of the flue, and boot of the reed pipes, pass through the pipe-rack holes. These fit tightly when in position.

Arrangement of the Pipes

The arrangement of the pipes, varies in different kinds of organs. In the Great Organ, the flue pipes stand in front, with the reed pipes behind. The largest flue pipes, such as the Open Diapason, are placed first. The others are arranged according to their size; the smallest, which are the mixtures, being placed next to the reeds.

The inside Choir Organ has its pipes arranged just opposite to the above plan, with the reed pipes in front, and the flue pipes behind.

In the Swell Organ also, the reeds are usually placed in front, and the flue pipes behind. The arrangement of the pipes is carried out in this manner for the convenience of the tuner, and in the Swell Organ it does not interfere with the freedom of the tone, as would the larger flue pipes, if they were placed in front. Pedal pipes have the same arrangement, and for like reasons.

Keys

The keys of the organ are usually made of white pine.

Thumping-Board

The thumping-board, which lies across the keys, is weighted with lead, and covered on the under side with felt.

This thumping-board is to prevent the keys from springing beyond their proper level, when the pressure of the finger is removed.

The Fan-frame Movement
(See Figure 6, 7 to 9, page 34)

The lower end of the sticker rests on the end of the key. The front end of the back-fall rests on the upper end of the sticker, while the other end is attached to the tracker. The tracker passes up and connects with the pull-down, which opens the pallet.

Backfall-Frame

A wooden frame, called the back-fall frame, holds the back-falls in their proper position. The frame itself is mortised to receive that portion of the back-fall above the center. Through the center of each back-fall is passed a strong piece of wire, which acts as a pivot.

Trackers

The trackers are thin strips of some light wood, such as pine, and are about three-eighths of an inch in width, one-eighth of an inch in thickness, and in length they vary from a few inches to as many feet as is required to reach the different wind-chests. Each tracker is provided at the lower end, with a threaded wire about three inches long, and which is fastened to it with glue and strong thread. At the upper end of the tracker there is fastened a hook of copper

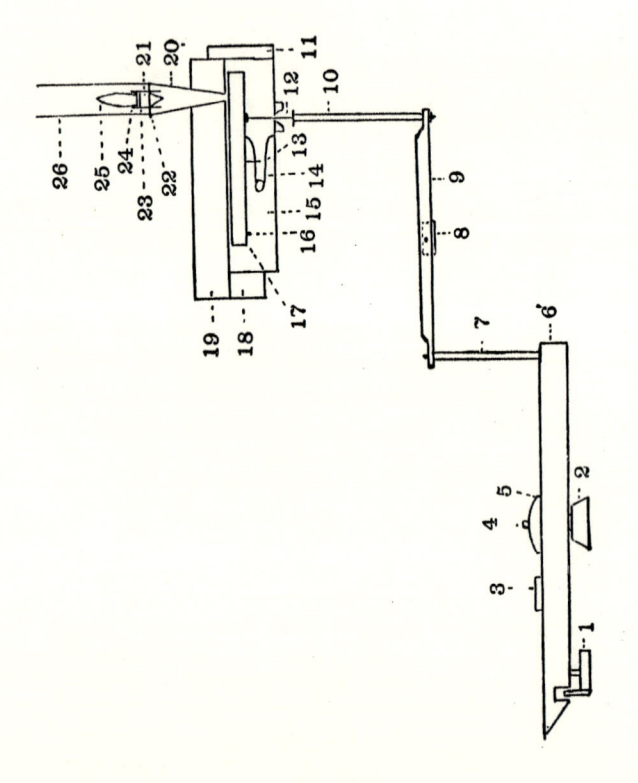

Fig. 6

wire, that communicates with the pull-down. The threaded wire at the lower end, is passed through a small hole in the end of the back-fall, and secured by a leather nut or button.

The Action of the Key Movement
(See Figure 6, 1 to 12, page 34.)

On pressing down the key, which is pivoted to the pin-rail, the back end of the key rises, lifting with it the sticker. This in turn raises the front end of the back-fall, which, by moving on the wire of the back-fall frame, causes the back end to descend. In doing so it draws down the tracker which lowers the valve.

Thus the compressed air in the wind-chest is allowed to escape through the valve-hole or groove into such pipes as the arrangement of the sliders permits. It is in passing through these pipes that the sound is produced.

The Sounding-Board

A sounding-board is always wider than the manual, and sometimes extends to twice its width or even more. Therefore it is evident that the grooves, instead of being in line with their respective keys, are, with few exceptions, more or less out of alignment with them. As it is necessary that the back end of each back-fall should be under its own groove, and at the same time have its front end rest on its proper sticker, under the above conditions all the back-falls, with the exception of a few in the center, are made to diverge, until in the extreme ones the back end is considerably out of line with the front. This fan-frame movement as it is called, owes its name to the arrangement of the back-falls.

Rollers

In some cases, as in the bass octave, the pipes are placed at one end of the sounding-board, while the corresponding keys are at the other. In order to connect these pipes, with their own pallets and corresponding keys, a rod or roller is provided for each key, and this extending along between the back-falls transfers the motion to the requisite pallet.

These rollers are each provided with two arms, one being directly over the back end of the back-fall, the other directly under the pallet.

The tracker wire in this case, instead of being a single wire is divided, one part connecting the back-fall and one roller arm, the other the second arm and the pallet. The rollers vary in length, from one inch to five feet: they are usually arranged one over the other, and are supported by pins, one in each end, which pass into studs. These studs stand out from a large board or frame, which is placed beneath the wind-chest, and reaches nearly the entire width of the sounding-board. This is called the roller-board movement.

Fig. 7.

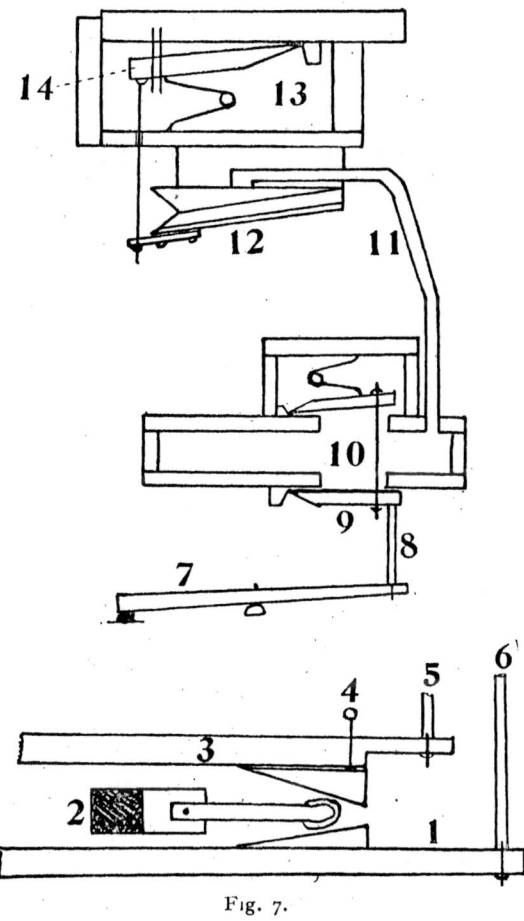

In the case of the Swell and Choir Organs, the back-fall frame is dispensed with, the movement of the keys being continued by the use of rollers, trackers and squares. The trackers transmit the movement horizontally, perpendicularly, or diagonally, and if very long, as in some cases reaching ten or twelve feet, they are supported by bridges. The bridges also keep them from striking each other.

Squares

The squares transfer the motion around corners. They are usually made of two pieces of wood, called arms, which are about three inches long and are dove-tailed together, to form a right angle.

The frame in which these squares work is termed the square-frame. The squares are sustained in this frame by small metal rods.

Couplers
(See Figure 7, 1 to 6, page 37.)

A coupler is an appliance uniting the different manuals, thus making new combinations and effects possible. Couplers are divided into two classes; manual couplers, and pedal couplers.

The first manual couplers, are commonly formed of a set of short stickers, one to each key, reaching from the upper surface of the Great Organ key to the under surface of the Swell key. These stickers pass through a bridge extending over the Great Organ key-board, from one side to the other, between the center and tail of the keys, and between the two manuals. This bridge is controlled by the coupler stop. When this is drawn on, the stickers are placed directly under the regulating button, and the Swell keys are thus connected with the Great keys.

The Pedal Couplers

As the pedals are lower than the keys of the manuals, it is necessary to use rollers resembling those in the key movement, having one arm over the pedal, and the other directly under the key with which it is connected. The pedal now having been brought into line with the key, a back-fall is used running underneath and parallel to the key. Between each back-fall and key there is a sticker. A pin in the lower end of each sticker connects it with the back-fall. The other end of the sticker is free to be moved forward or backward as the stop is drawn or thrown off. The stickers pass through a bridge which moves with the stop and carries the stickers with it.

The Draw-Stop Action

The draw-stop action consists of the following parts: lable, stop-head, stop-rod, trundle or square, trace and lever.

The label indicates the quality and pitch of tone. The figures on the stop label 32, 16, 8, 4 and 2 feet refer to the length and pitch of the pipe. If an organ has a 32 feet set, and open pipes are used the longest or lowest pipe will measure 32 feet in length;

and if a 2 feet set is used the longest or lowest pipe of this set will measure 2 feet; this same relation exists for the other sets between those mentioned.

The stop-head is connected with the stop-rod, which is the rod carrying the motion to the trundle, or with the square, if the trundle is not used, and which conveys the motion around an angle. The trundle consists of two arms and a rod. The trace continues the motion at right angles with the draw stop-rod. The lever conveys the motion upwards to the slider.

When the Stop Draws too Far

A stop-rod will sometimes come out too far or return too far. This is caused by the connecting pin at one of the centers having worked out; it may occur either at the end of the stop-rod that connects with one arm of the square, or where the second arm connects with the trace; also where the trace connects with the lever. All that is necessary to remedy this is to replace the old pin or provide a new one.

When the Stop Draws too Hard

Sometimes a stop-rod will draw very hard, this is usually caused by the moisture in the atmosphere swelling the upper-board and slider, thus causing them to press against each other and thereby producing friction. This can be remedied by loosening the screws that fasten down the upper-board; these screws, in the winter months, when the air is heated, will have to be tightened again. At times when the air is heated a stop-rod will draw hard. This is caused by the upper-board or slider being warped. In this case if the screws have to be loosened so much as to cause a running of air, the only remedy will be to remove the upper-board and take out the slider, in order to free the parts that bind.

When a slider is supported with a rail at the stop-lever end, and the rail bears too hard against the slider, thereby causing the stop to draw hard, it can be remedied by removing the rail and cutting away that portion of it which interferes with the action of the slider.

The Dip

The dip of the manuals will sometimes become too shallow or too deep; which will result in the pipes of the organ sounding out of tune. The cause of this change in the dip is hot, dry air in the winter, and hot damp air in the summer. In the winter months the dip will become shallow, in the summer months too deep. The reason for this is that the heat by drying and contracting the frame and key-movements lessens the dip, and dampness expands it by swelling the parts. The dip is regulated by means of thumb screws placed over the back-fall frame of each manual.

The Tremolo

The tremolo is set in motion in the following manner: the stop opens the valve and allows the air to pass in, thus setting the valve in motion. The valve is thrown back by a spring, the strength of which exactly counterbalances the pressure of air. These two opposing forces, the wind on the inside and the spring on the outside, give a trembling motion to the air. The tremolo apparatus is fastened to one of the sides of the wind-trunk. Besides the tremolo, there are other effects of forte, piano, diminuendo, and crescendo which are attainable from the Swell Organ.

Detailed Action of the Tracker Organ
(See Figure 6, page 34.)

The separate parts are as follows:
1. *Front Rail.* This rail is covered on top with a continuous piece of felt, or punchings, to prevent the keys from coming into noisy contact with the rail.
2. *Center rail.*
3. *Thumping-Board.* This board prevents the keys from springing above their natural position when they are released. The board is loaded with lead, and has its under side covered with felt.
4. *Center pin.* This pin acts as a pivot on which the key works.
5. *Key Button.* The button prevents the key from making too much side motion.
6. *Key.*
7. *Sticker.* The sticker transmits the

motion from the key to the front end of the back-fall.
8. *Back-fall Frame.* The frame to which are pinned the back-falls.
9. *Back-fall.* At the back end of the back-fall is fastened the tracker.
10. *Tracker.*
11. *Bung.*
12. *Pull-down Wire.* The pull-down wire is fastened to the tracker.
13. *Direction Pins.* These pins guide the pallet in its descent and ascent.
14. *Pallet-Spring.* This spring, with the aid of the compressed air in the wind-chest, closes the pallet.
15. *Wind-Chest.*
16. *Pallet Pin.*
17. *Pallet.* The upper end of the pull-down wire is connected with the pallet, by means of a hook which opens the latter, and allows the compressed air to pass up to the pipe, and make it speak.
18. *Wind-Bar.*
19. *Sounding-board.*
20. *Pipe-foot.*
21. *Mouth.*
22. *Lower Lip.*
23. *Upper Lip.*
24. *Ear.*
25. *Leaf.*
26. *Body.*

Tracker Action

Notwithstanding the fact that the touch of large tracker organs is very heavy, nevertheless the tracker organ has its advantages. The organist can operate the action of small organs very well, but in large organs it is almost impossible to display great technique since the key is attached directly to the pallet in the wind-chest, and this makes the key go down correspondingly hard. The tracker action is also very noisy as compared with the tubular and electric actions. A favorable feature, however, is the fact that the action does not easily get out of order, while the pneumatic and the electric actions require much more attention, and are in general much less reliable than the tracker action.

The Sound-Producing Portion of the Organ

The sound of an organ is produced from a collection of pipes, which are made either of tin, zinc, lead or wood. They are round or square, long or short, broad or narrow, according to circumstances.

Tin is superior to all other substances for the use of organ pipes. It recommends itself by its great durability, superior silver color, lightness and flexibility. Pipes made of this material are not liable to be attacked by the strong acid in the wood of the upper-boards that support them. This acid will eat away the lower part of pipes which are made chiefly of lead. Tin is less susceptible to change of temperature than are many of the compounds used. On account of the hardness of tin, pipes made of this material stand much longer in tune. In weight tin is one-third lighter than lead. Material is called tin, as long as the proportion of alloy is sufficiently small to improve the whole, which is considered to be the case when the alloy does not exceed more than one-third of the whole weight of the metal.

Spotted Metal Pipes

Pipes containing this admixture of material are said to produce the greatest amount of tone, the quality of which is bright and full. If pipes were made of pure tin the tone would have a tendency to be rather piercing; for this reason the tin alloy is preferred. If the metal pipes are spotted, it proves that they are made of alloyed tin, as these spots indicate that about two-thirds tin was used.

Lead alone or with a slight mixture of tin, is almost worthless as a material for organ pipes. It is naturally so soft and heavy that the foot of the pipe is liable to become depressed, and the languid to sink, whereby the intonation of the pipe is endangered if not destroyed.

The Detection of Poor Metal

Poor metal is detected in the following ways: it has a dark blue tint; if struck it will produce a dull hollow sound; and it is easily scratched, while tin cannot readily be marked in that manner. If paper be rubbed upon a pipe made chiefly of lead, the paper will become soiled.

The Preparation of Metal

The metal for organ pipes is prepared by putting the different materials together in a crucible and melting them: the compound thus obtained is cast into a sheet, by pouring it, while in a fluid state, into a wooden trough. The trough is then pushed along a bench covered with linen cloth, the metal escaping from the trough through a narrow opening at the back, and leaving a layer of metal behind it as it moves forward. The wider the opening the thicker will be the sheet of metal produced. After being cast, the sheet is planed down to the exact thickness required.

Pipes of Various Shapes

Organ pipes are of various shapes. Round pipes maintain the same body diameter throughout the whole length. There are three varieties of such pipes, the open, the stopped, and the half-stopped.

The open pipes are the most numerous in all organs. They are called open Diapason, Principal, Fifteenth, and Mixture. The stopped pipes, have the top closed or covered with metal; such are the Stopped Diapason and Gedackt. The half-stopped pipes are such as the Chimney Flute.

The Parts of Wooden Pipes

Wooden pipes are formed of the following parts: body, block, throat between the block and the cap, foot, upper and lower lip, and mouth.

How the Sound is Produced

The sound of a metal flue pipe is produced by the admission of a current of wind at the toe of the pipe, and which, rushing upward passes through the wind-way and strikes against the upper lip. This produces a concussion which prevents the air from issuing in a continuous manner from the mouth, and causes it to proceed intermittently. The periodical motion of the air thus caused, is communicated to the column of air within the body of the pipe, and this air being set in motion a sound is produced.

A wooden flue pipe is made to sound in much the same manner as a metal pipe of the same kind. The wind on being admitted passes up through the pipe-foot into the throat, and from there into the hollowed part of the cap into which it forces itself. After passing through the wind-way between the upper edge of the cap and block, the wind strikes against the upper lip and is thus made to vibrate, and these vibrations are communicated to the body of the pipe.

Pipes Furnished with Ears and Beard

Wooden flue pipes are sometimes furnished with ears on each side of the mouth, and in some cases with a cross piece fastened on beneath the under lip, and technically called a beard. Ears and beards are attached especially to pipes of very narrow scale or small mouths.

These additions keep the wind from spreading, and also quicken the speech of the pipe. If the ears are very large they are made use of for the purpose of tuning.

Length of Stopped Pipes

A stopped flue pipe of a given length will produce a sound as low as that of an open pipe twice its length. This fact is accounted for in this way. The vibrations instead of escaping at the top of the shorter pipe, as they do in the case of the longer, are checked by the stopper that closes the end of the shorter pipe. As a result of this the vibrations are turned back again down the pipe before they can make their escape, which they do through the mouth.

The vibrations of the stopped pipe therefore travel a distance equal to that of the open pipe, hence the pitch will be the same. For instance a stopped pipe of two feet, will give the same sound as an open one of four feet. A stopped pipe of four feet in length, will give the same sound as an open pipe of eight feet.

A stopped pipe of the same length and diameter will not speak the true octave below the open pipe, but it gives instead a major seventh.

A stopped pipe must be a trifle larger in diameter than the open, to speak the true octave, and in the proportion of one-sixteenth to seven-sixteenths.

Character of Tone Influenced by Dimensions

The size and dimensions of a metal flue pipe exert a great influence on the strength, character, and quality of the tone of the pipe. The dimensions however are subject to more or less change. The width of the mouth is one-fourth the circumference of the body, and the height one-fourth the width. Measuring according to this the mouth of a pipe sixteen inches in circumference, is four inches in width and one in height.

Some pipes have a wider mouth than this. Others a narower one; some a higher and some a lower. A pipe with a wide high mouth will produce a round powerful tone; a high and narrow mouth a sharp tone, and a narrow and low mouth a delicate tone. But even these different shaped mouths have their limits: for if the mouth of a pipe be cut too high, it will be slow of speech, if it speak at all; and if a mouth be too narrow the pipe will speak its octave.

The greatest deviations are found in the wooden stopped pipes, the mouths of which in those of small scale are equal in height to one-half or two-thirds their width; while large scale stopped pipes are sometimes just the opposite, and have very low mouths.

Voicing

The voicing of a pipe consists of the careful adjustment of its mouth, setting the upper and lower lip, closing or opening the toe, to govern the amount of wind to be admitted, conveying the wind through the wind-way in a sheet of the exact thickness. The wind passing through the wind-way must strike the upper lip fairly, and not in or out. Thus following out the necessary details to give true speech and character of tone to the pipe.

The notches or nicks are those small marks or cuts on the languid and lower lip of a pipe, which resemble the edge of a saw; they are coarse or fine according to the tone character of the pipe. The open Diapason will receive a coarser nick than the Dulciana.

The nick of the eight foot open Diapason is one-sixteenth of an inch deep, and these nicks are cut at intervals of one-eighth of an inch. These nicks are less deep, as the upper end of the scale is reached, and are fewer in number.

In regard to voicing a metal pipe, as far as the eye can detect it consists principally in the nicety with which the nicks are cut in the languid and lower lip of the pipe. The nicks are cut on the lower edge of the languid, and the notches on the lower lip.

Nicks and notches run parallel with each other, and sometimes, though not always, at an angle with the body of the pipe. A pipe that has few nicks will produce a round sonorous tone; and one that is regularly nicked, a much softer and more musical tone. The deeper the nick the more harsh or reedy the tone. Nicks are deepest in the languid.

A wooden flue pipe is voiced by filing small grooves or nicks on the surface or face of the block. These nicks run almost at right angles to the upper lip, and are deepest and widest at the mouth, and gradually run out on the plane surface of the block. This block is nicked before the cap is put on, its upper edge is also beveled opposite the under lip, in order to direct the wind against the upper lip. If it be beveled too much or too little, the pipe will be slow in speech, or off of voice, if it speaks at all.

The wind-way will now have to be adjusted, by making the lower lip an equal distance from the languid. The wind-hole for the Open Diapason should be three-fourths of an inch in diameter, and there is a gradual reduction to one-eighth of an inch in the highest pipe.

The width of the mouth of a pipe is about one-fourth that of its circumference, and its height is about one-fourth that of its width.

The height of mouth and size of wind-way, as well as the scale and pressure of wind, regulate the nicking. A slight increase of power should be given to all the stops of the treble, to give the effect of a crescendo from the bass up.

The nicks in the languid and lower lip, run parallel; those in the languid being made the deeper of the two. The number of nickers used in nicking a set of Diapason pipes is four.

The voicers art can disguise or even reverse the quality of tone.

The scale of a pipe is its dimensions; for example:

Length of C pipe.	Width of mouth.
Eight ft.	Five inches.
Four ft.	Two and ten-twelfths in.
Two ft.	One and five-eighths in.
One ft.	One inch.
Top C.	Nine-sixteenths of an in.

How a Pipe Vibrates

After the wind has been admitted into the foot of the pipe, it rushes through the windway in a thin sheet, which is directed against the upper lip. The mouth or space between the upper and lower lip now being covered with this current of air, the stream of air covering the mouth is exposed on the outside to the pressure of the atmosphere, while on the inside it is protected from it by the body of the pipe.

The atmospheric air that passes out through the mouth of the pipe, is forced upwards and against the burnished part of the pipe, which results in an inward draught beneath, and through the mouth. This inward moving draught on the outside of the mouth being stronger than the air at rest within the pipe, the sheet of wind passing through the wind-way gives way for an instant, and the inward bearing draught breaks through, and passes into the pipe, which is immediately overcome by the power of the sheet of wind. This in its turn is most powerful until the draught overpowers it again, which produces a periodical movement of the air against the upper lip of the pipe. This periodical movement of the air takes place with greater or less rapidity, corresponding to the proportions of the mouth, and pressure of wind, which sets in motion the column of air in the body of the pipe. The elastic action of the lower end of the column of air in that portion of the mouth aids, by compression and expansion, in restoring in turns the sheet of wind and inward bearing draught.

Pitch of Flue Pipes

The pitch of a flue pipe depends therefore as much upon the number of vibrations that take place at the mouth of the pipe in a second of time, as upon the number of vibrations that occur in the body of the pipe in the same time, and with which no doubt the latter agrees. This accounts for the fact that if a pipe be shortened it requires more wind than before in order to increase the vibrations at the mouth, so that they may correspond with the quicker vibrations that take place in the body of the pipe.

Pipes Speaking Their Octave or Fifth

Although the length of the vibrating column of air may be to a certain extent made longer or shorter with but little effect on the speech, yet if the length be very great in relation to its diameter, and in proportion to its mouth, the vibration of the mouth will be too fast to agree with the slower vibrations of the lengthened column of air. As a result the pipe will take its octave or will not speak at all. It is owing to this increased length, with a narrow mouth in proportion to the body, that Dulciana pipes, usually the smallest in the scale of open flue pipes, are so liable to speak their octaves, if at all out of order.

Pipes speaking their octave or fifth, can be remedied by slightly closing the toe of the pipe, or by pressing in the upper lip. Before making any change in the pipe, it must be thoroughly cleaned, as dust and cobwebs collect in the pipe, thereby causing the above defects. In opening and closing the wind-way, use a flat, thin piece of wood; as wood is not nearly so likely as iron to damage the nicking on the lip and languid.

Wind-way Too Deep

If the wind-way be made too deep, the current of air will be too thick, and will prevent the inward bearing draught from breaking through, and the pipe will not speak with full strength, or will only produce a dull hissing sound. If the mouth be cut too high, the current of air will not fully cover the space between the upper and lower lips, or the air will not reach across the mouth, which will cause the speech of the pipe to be weak and wavering.

Mouth of Wooden Pipes

Wooden pipes of four-square shape, have a mouth as broad as the inside of the pipe on which it is cut. Its height is about one-fourth that of its width, but as wooden pipes are sometimes of oblong shape, the mouth is often cut on the narrow side, while in others it is on the broad side. It is evident therefore that the mouth of a wooden pipe is subject to a great deal more change than that of a metal pipe.

Tone Influenced by Thick Metal or Wood

If the body of a metal flue pipe is thick and elastic, the tone will be firm, clear and distinct. The same result is obtained from a wooden pipe made of such material as hard wood or oak, as these give the strongest and clearest tones. Whereas, if soft wood or pine is used, a mellow tone is produced. The tone of a large open metal pipe is clear and sonorous, while that of an open wooden pipe is thick and heavy.

Reed Pipes Placed on a Heavier Wind

Reed pipes will speak with more power if placed on a heavier wind, than will the flue pipes.

The Parts of Reed Pipes

A reed pipe consists of the following parts; block, tuning wire, tube or body, boot, reed, tongue, metal or wooden wedge, and bell.

In casting the block of the reed pipe, there are two round holes left; in the larger of these, the reed and tongue are fastened with a wedge, and through this reed the air passes from the boot to the body of the pipe. The smaller hole in the block that is a little in front of the larger one, receives the tuning wire that is required to regulate the exact length of the vibrating portion of the tongue.

The block rests on the upper edge of the boot.

How the Tongue Vibrates

The reed is a small tube made of brass, and is usually made widest at the lower end. In the front is left an opening over which the tongue is placed, which latter is set in vibration by the air passing through this opening into the body of the pipe.

How the Tongue is Fastened

The tongue is a thin elastic piece of tempered brass, and is fastened at the upper end with a small metal or wooden wedge; it is also slightly curved upwards from the tuning wire to the toe. The portion that vibrates is below the tuner, and can be lengthened or shortened as required.

Kinds of Reeds

There are four kinds of reeds. The open reeds which extend all the way up, have more power and admit more wind than the closed, which are but partially open, and therefore more quiet.

Reeds Free

In the free reed the tongue passes through the reed, and vibrates by cutting off the air; and the tone thus produced is as smooth and continuous as that of a flue pipe.

Reeds Striking

In the striking reed, the tongue strikes the reed, which makes the tone more powerful than that of the free reed, and causes a clattering sound with the tone. This peculiar quality is due to the beating of the tongue against the reed.

A thin tongue gives a thin harsh tone, while a thick one yields the reverse. Thick tongued reeds stand in tune better than thin ones.

A reed tongue must lie perfectly flat on a flat surface, when held at one end and pressed down at the other. A tongue made of hard tempered brass will give a harsher tone than one having a softer temper.

The part of the metal plate which is to form the neck of the tube is made much thicker than the other end which is to support the pipe.

Body In Unison With Tongue

If the tube or body of a reed pipe is in unison with the tongue, the tone will be more musical, although it is possible to produce a tone if they are not in unison. But it will not be as full and of as good quality.

Character of Reed Tone

Short bodied pipes give a light tone. If pipes of inverted conical tubes are used the tone is sonorous: if they are narrow the tone is rather thin, and nasal, as in bassoon pipes.

If a bell be placed on the top of the pipe the tone becomes more clear. The strength of the tone also depends upon the shape and size of the opening in the reed, upon the material of which the tongue is made, whether it is simply composed of brass, or contains a mixture of copper and brass, and upon the equal thickness, and thinness of the tongue, on its curvature, as well as upon the smoothness and flatness of the edges of the reed, against which the tongue strikes.

Intonation of Tone

The Clarionet, Oboe, and Bassoon are reed pipes of delicate intonation. Their tongues are long, thin and narrow. Those of strong, full and powerful tone, as the Horn and Trumpet have broader, thicker and shorter tongues.

Vibration of Reed Tongues

The tongue of a reed, when in a state of rest is slightly curved upward, this allows the air to rush through the opening in the reed drawing the tongue with it; when this opening is closed the tongue springs back again, thus causing it to vibrate.

Pitch of Reed and Flue Pipe

The pitch of a reed pipe depends upon the number of beats or vibrations of the tongue in a second of time. In that of a flue pipe the pitch depends upon the length of the body of the pipe or on the length of the column of air in the body of the pipe, which is governed by the following laws: By doubling the length the pitch is lowered an octave; by halving it, it is raised an octave.

If the pitch of a reed pipe is more than four or five beats sharp or flat, and the temperature is above 70 degrees F. or below 60 degrees F. it is best to tune the pipe at the top, as this favors its tone.

Table of Vibrations in Flue and Reed Pipes

The following table shows the number of vibrations in a flue pipe, also the number of blows of the tongue in a reed pipe in a second of time, from sub C_2 to two-lined C ".

Note of C	Vibrations in the flue pipe	Blows of tongue in the reed pipe	Length of the open flue pipe
CCCC	16.	16.	32. feet
CCC	32.	32.	16. "
CC	64.	64.	8. "
Tenor or small C	128.	128.	4. "
Middle or One-lined C'	256.	256.	2. "
Two-lined C"	512.	512.	1. foot

The above are complete vibrations. The body of a reed pipe gives to the reed the character required, also the necessary strength.

Extreme Length of Organ Pipes

Organ flue pipes vary a great deal in size. The longest speaking pipe is thirty-two feet long, and the shortest is three-quarters of an inch. In this measurement the foot of the pipe is not taken into consideration, as that is simply a support and wind conveyance, to the pipe.

Compass of Pipes

The difference in pitch of the two pipes just mentioned is nine octaves. Therefore if we include all the semitones between these pipes, we have a series of one hundred and nine different sizes. Pipes are not always just as long as above stated, but this is somewhere near the average, as a greater wind, or a higher or lower pitch, will change the length.

Pitch Changed According to Stops Used

The organ differs a great deal from other instruments in the fact that there is not a fixed pitch for each key, but from eight to ten different sounds can be produced from any separate key, according to the stops drawn.

Table Giving Names of Octaves

The following table gives the names of the different octaves from sub C to six-lined C '''''':

The thirty-two foot, or sub C. The length of this pipe is thirty-two feet. Its sound is lower than any other musical instrument. It is called thirty-two foot C, on account of its length; or four C, and is marked CCCC. The pitch of this pipe is one octave below the lowest C of the piano.

The sixteen foot or contra C. The pitch of this C is in unison with the lowest C of the piano. It is called the three C, and is marked CCC.

The eight foot, or great C. The pitch of this C is in unison with the open fourth string of the Violoncello. It is called the double C, and is marked CC.

The four foot, or small C. The pitch of this C is in unison with the lowest C, of the Viola. It is sometimes called tenor C.

The two foot, one-lined or middle C'. The pitch of this C is in unison with the lowest C of the flute. The reason why this is called middle C, is, that it was placed on the middle line of the ancient great or grand staff of eleven lines.

The one foot or two-lined C". This is in unison with the lowest C of the piccolo.

The C of six inches,—three-lined C'''. The C of three inches,—four-lined C''''. The C of one and one-half inches,—five-lined C'''''. This is the highest pitch on the piano. The C of three-quarters of an inch,—six-lined C'''''', which is the smallest pipe made.

The range of vibrations of the piano tuned to International pitch is from about 27 to 4136

The range of the violin, 193 to 2068.

The range of the average human voice, from 82 to 1044: this is the whole range from bass to soprano, inclusive.

The range of the organ, is from about 16 to 8272, or from sub C to six-lined C⁗́.

The Scale of Organ Pipes

By the scale of an organ, is meant the width or narrowness of a pipe in relation to its length, a pipe is said to be of either large or small scale, if its body is large or small as compared with its length. If the diameter of a pipe is carried to its full extent as compared with its full length it is said to be of large scale. While the opposite is true if it is small as compared with its length.

The length of pipe that will sound middle C is much larger and shorter in the open Diapason than that of the Dulciana, which is longer and narrower for the same sound or pitch. The difference in the length of these pipes, is due to the narrowness of the one as compared with the other.

If the above pipes were of the same length with no difference in diameter there would be a difference in the pitch of the pipes. The following will explain the above stated conditions, which is based on two foot or middle C:

Diameter of Flue Pipes

Name of Pipe.	Diameter at Mouth.	Diameter at Top.	Length.
Open Diapason.	2, 7-24 in.	2, 7-24 in.	1 ft. 10, 3-4 in.
Dulciana.	1, 3-8 "	1, 3-8 "	1 " 11, 5-8 "
Gamba.	1, 1-2 "	1, 1-2 "	2 " 3-6 "
Gemshorne.	2, 1-8 "	2, 17-24 "	1 " 11, 1-2 "

Diameter of Reed Pipes

Name of Pipe.	Diameter at top.	Length.
Clarionet.	1, 1-24 in.	1 ft. 1, 1-2 in.
Bassoon.	1, 1-4 "	1 " 8 "
Oboe.	2, 1-6 "	1 " 8, 1-4 "
Trumpet.	2, 5-6 "	1 " 8, 3-4 "
Horn.	3, 1-3 "	1 " 9 "

Diapason Work

Stops belonging to the Diapason work are the Open Diapason, Principal, Twelfth, and Fifteenth.

Closed Work

The closed work are: the Stopped Diapason, Stopped Flute, and Stopped Piccolo.

Mutation Stops

Mutation Stops are such as do not correspond in pitch with the keys touched. The Twelfth and Tierce.

Compound Stops

By compound Stops is understood an assemblage of several pipes, three, four, five or more to each key, all speaking at the same time.

Largest Manual Stop

The Sub-Bourdon, the largest manual stop used, is a thirty-two foot tone, and is only used in very large organs. Its compass is to middle C.

The Double Open Diapason, is of sixteen feet length on the manual, and thirty-two feet on the pedal.

The Open Diapason is a stop of eight feet length on the manual, and sixteen feet on the pedal. It is called Open Diapason to distinguish it from the closed or stopped Diapason.

Diapason Stop Taken as a Standard

The Diapason is taken for the standard or scale, of the organ, and all other pipes are made with reference to it. The Diapason therefore exerts its influence through all the stops.

Name of Stops, and Description of Tone

The Dulciana is an eight foot stop, soft and delicate in tone.

The Stopped Diapason or Gedäckt, which means stopped, is an eight foot stop, mild and fluty in tone.

The Clarabella is an eight foot stop, heavy, powerful and fluty in tone.

The Gamba is an eight foot stop, pungent, and somewhat imitating the Cello in tone, it is rather slow in speech.

The Keraulophon is an eight foot stop, soft, delicate and reedy in tone; the peculiar character of this tone is obtained by boring a small hole in the body or cap of the pipe, near the top.

The Open Diapason is the quickest and fullest in speech of all the above pipes.

The Octave or Principal is a four foot stop, clear and full in tone.

The Flute is a four foot stop, representing the tone of the wind instrument after which it is named.

The Twelfth is a stop of two and two-thirds feet in length; in pitch it is a perfect fifth above the octave, or a twelfth above the Diapason.

The Fifteenth is a stop of two feet in length; in pitch it is an octave above the Octave, or a fifteenth above the Diapason.

The Piccolo is a stop of two feet in length, bright and piercing in tone, and is in unison with the fifteenth.

The Mixture consists of from two to five ranks of pipes, such as the twelfth, fifteenth, seventeenth, nineteenth, twenty-second, twenty-sixth, and twenty-ninth, from the ground tone.

The Trumpet is a stop of eight feet in length, powerful and penetrating in tone, resembling that of the wind instrument after which it is named.

The Cornopean is an eight foot stop, full and loud in tone, which is richer than that of the Trumpet.

The Oboe is an eight foot stop, thin and soft in tone, resembling the wind instrument after which it is named.

The Clarionet is an eight foot stop, rich and full in tone.

The Vox Humana is an eight foot stop, intended to imitate the human voice, and is usually placed in the swell organ.

Length of Pipes with Reference to Harmonic Series

According to the scale of the Pipe Organ, with reference to the harmonic series, the length of pipes would be as follows: If the eight feet tone is used for the foundation, the next would be four feet or one-half; then two feet and two-thirds, or one third; two feet or one-fourth; one and three-fifths of a foot, or one fifth; one and one-third foot, or one sixth; and one foot, or one eighth.

If it were not for the above lengths of pipes, the tone of the organ would be thin and dull, as in all stopped pipes the tone is simple.

Until equal temperament was used, keys with more than three flats, or sharps were seldom made use of. By means of equal temperament the most wolfish key, A flat Major, has been changed to one of the most pleasing.

Bach tuned his own Clavichord and Harpsichord by means of equal temperament.

Reasons for Organs' Ciphering

There may be something hard on the pallet which will prevent its closing. The pallet spring may be too weak. The pallet may be caught on the direction pins. The sheep-skin may be either loose or warped.

How the Pallets are Covered

Pallets are covered with two thicknesses of soft sheep-skin and the shiny surface is glued to the pallet; this surface will have to be roughened to make the glue hold, a small hack saw is best suited for this work, and drawing the teeth of the saw sideways over the skin will roughen it. A very thin coating of glue is put on the pallet; this is to prevent the use of too much glue which would harden the skin. The second piece of skin is glued to the top of the first and in the same manner. When the glue is set, trim the leather to the edges of the pallet. The soft surface of the sheep-skin that comes in contact with the groove should have its pores well filled with whiting, thus insuring a tight joint.

The pull-down wire may become rusted, which will cause it to bind in the brass plate through which it passes. Or the bung rail may be too narrow, thus allowing the end of the pallet to catch against its side. Remedy: Take out the bung, remove the rail and place heavy pieces of card-board between the bung and rail.

Reasons for Ciphering caused by the Key Movement

Melted candle grease may have dropped between the keys. This may be remedied by scraping away the tallow with a knife.

Some small substance, such as pins or small beads, may be wedged between the keys. To remedy this raise one key while the other is lowered, at the same time separating them, without too much force, in order to free the obstruction.

The key may have become warped. To remedy this the key must be taken out, and the warped surface planed level. To take out the key remove the thumping-board and Great and Swell key stickers.

The sticker may bind in passing through the bridge, or the black lead may be worn from the sticker. The back-fall may slip off the sticker under a heavy blow, and catch on the sticker pin; or there may be grit or dirt in the pin holes of some part of the key movement.

The buttons of the pull-downs may be too tight. A pedal spring may be broken, thus causing the weight of the pedal to lower the key a trifle, when the coupler is on: when the coupler is thrown off the ciphering will cease.

A Running of Air

This is one of the most perplexing defects that can exist, as it usually occurs in the most hidden part of the sounding-board. Its presence is shown by the sounding of a second pipe, or ciphering if there is only one or more stops drawn, as there is not air enough passing through this leakage, if there are a sufficient number of stops drawn, to allow ciphering.

A running may be caused in the following ways: By an upper-board not being screwed down; this is remedied by tightening the screws. It is sometimes caused by a leakage from one groove to the next, or a sounding-board bar may have sprung, or become slightly separated from the table. The sounding-board bar itself may be checked or cracked, which will allow a little wind to pass to the next groove. This may be remedied, by gluing a piece of sheep-skin over the crack; although some will resort to bleeding which is not wise.

Humming Caused by Slider

In the old styled organs there is sometimes a humming caused by one slider rubbing against the next as it is drawn, this opens the second a little, allowing the wind to pass into the pipes of the second stop. This can be remedied, by fixing a wooden pin between the sliders, or by planing the edge of one of them.

Cause of Low Dull Sound

In some organs where the pipes are very close together, so that the wind passes out of the mouth of one pipe and enters that of another, there is produced a low dull sound. In some cases this can be remedied by turning the mouth of one pipe in a different direction, or by placing one of them on a longer foot.

Defects in the Key Movement

Sometimes a key will go down half way without sounding, after which it will go down with a snap. This is caused by the roller being too weak and thus twists or springs for a time. The remedy for this is stronger rollers. In some old styled organs a key will at first resist the touch until the pressure is increased, when it will give way, causing a sharp noise. This is caused by the roller arms being made of iron instead of wood, as roller arms made of iron will rust.

Sometimes a thumping will be heard as the keys go down. This is caused by the felt on the front-rail becoming hard or too thin, and can be remedied by putting on a new piece.

In old organs where the iron arms and metal tracker were used there was a good deal of noise and squeaking, which has been remedied by the use of wooden arms and leather buttons or nuts for the tracker wire. Sometimes a squeaking is caused by roller pins, also by pull-down wires where they pass through brass plate. In a long key-movement extention, there is sometimes a noise caused by the trackers striking together; this is remedied by the use of another bridge, although this will increase the friction of the action a trifle, unless reels are used, which will not interfere with the touch.

Leveling Keys

Sometimes a key will be too low or out of line, this is caused by some part of the key movement having slipped, such as the tracker wires being broken, or the roller arms becoming unglued or broken; it is also caused by the button slipping down the threaded wire of the tracker, which cause is most frequent, and is remedied either by the use of a new button, or turning back the old one; the former is the better way. In turning back this button the tracker should be held firmly just above the threaded wire, to prevent breaking the tracker.

Sometimes a dumb key will be caused by the breaking of a square.

Ram Coupler (Tracker Organ)
(See Figure 7, page 37.)

1. Tail of great organ key. When the front of the key is lowered, the tail rises carrying with it the ram, which is pinned to the bridge marked 2. If this bridge is in position as shown in the illustration, the coupler stop Swell to Great, is on. The space between the upper surface of the Great key, and the under surface of the Swell key now being occupied, the Swell key is thus made to move with the Great.

2. Bridge. This bridge is controlled by the coupler stop. When the stop is off, it

places the bridge in such a position that the ram cannot fill the space between the Great and Swell key.

3. Tail of Swell key.

4. Regulating screw. This screw is used to regulate the distance between the ram and key. If the coupler does not lower the Swell key to its full depth, it will cause the pipe to sound out of tune. This fault is remedied by turning down the regulating screw. If the regulating screw is turned down too far, it will cause the key to cipher.

5. Swell sticker. Upper end of sticker connects with back-fall.

6. Great sticker. Upper end of sticker connects with back-fall.

Defects in the Bellows
(See Figure 4, page 16.)

The most common fault in a bellows, is that of squeaking. It is caused by the friction of the bellows-handle on its center, or a rubbing of the pump-rods with the lever of the feeders. This is remedied with a little grease.

Cause of a Moaning Sound

When the escape valve is fastened to the middle-board and is operated with a cord attached to the top-board, and when the bellows is full, the escape valve is liable to produce a moaning sound, in opening and closing. The cause of this is the valve rubbing against the spring block. It is remedied by gluing a piece of leather where valve comes in contact with block.

Cause of Clattering Sound

Sometimes a clattering is heard as the feeders are drawn up. This is caused by wooden valves covered with leather that has become hard, striking the bottom-board as they close. To remedy this, put in new leather valves.

Cause of Gasping Sound

Sometimes there is a gasping sound as a feeder descends. This is caused by the wind rushing through the valves, which are too few to supply the feeders. To remedy it, increase the number of valves.

Bellows Runs Down too Soon

During the winter months when the air is heated, a bellows will sometimes run down much sooner than at other times. This is caused by the pores of the wood being open, or the leather valves shrinking. It will usually remedy itself; if not, the valves will have to be repaired, and the pores of the wood closed with a few coats of shellac.

Bellows Effects Speech of Pipes

The working of the bellows will sometimes affect the speech of the pipe, by a slight wavering of the tone, when the feeders commence and complete their stroke. This is caused by the additional compression at that moment, particularly if the wind-trunks are too small, or if there is no concussion bellows.

Cause of Robbing

In some organs if a chord is held down with the right hand in the treble, and a chord is struck with the left, the treble pipes will weaken in speech. This is a sure indication that the wind-trunk or chest is too small. Sometimes certain stops sound full and bright when played alone, and flat or dull when used with others. This is serious and is caused by the grooves not holding wind enough to supply all the pipes; or the pallet holes are too small.

Robbing: How Tested

This robbing usually shows itself in the lower octave or octave and a half, and can be tested in the following way: by drawing the twelfth or fifteenth, and holding down one of the lower keys. The pipe will speak with full power, then by adding other stops, the tone will become flat. This proves that the grooves do not hold, or do not receive sufficient wind. The only remedy for this is larger grooves, with larger pallet-holes. In such a case the bass of the small stops, must be tuned with all stops drawn, which will counterbalance the robbing. Recently some are using two sounding-boards instead of one, which separates the treble from the bass, thus putting an end to all robbing.

Leakage

Sometimes there is an escape of wind, producing a hissing noise. This is caused by a slight leakage in the wind-trunk or chest.

The pull-down may also have worn an oblong hole in the brass plate. This can be remedied by gluing a piece of leather on the trunk; or if the leak is around the bung, by putting on a little thicker piece of leather; and if it is around the pull-down, then ream the hole and put in a size larger wire.

Pipes with a Weak Waving Tone

It very often happens, that small pipes are off speech, or their tone is weak and wavering, if they speak at all. This is caused by particles of dust between the languid and lower lip. To remedy it, wipe the languid, dust the nicking, and clear the wind-way.

Tone Uneven

Sometimes the tone of pipes is uneven. This may be caused by the upper and lower lips being placed in too far, or not in far enough. The languid may be too high, or too low; or the toe of the pipe may be either too large or too small.

Trembling Tone caused by Pipes being Crowded

Gamba's, Dulciana's and Keraulophon's are peculiarly liable to this defect. If a pipe is too crowded, by removing a few pipes that are nearest its mouth, the trembling will cease. Remedy: If possible turn the mouth in a different direction.

Trembling is sometimes caused by the pipe being loose. Remedy: Fasten the pipe to the rack boards provided for that purpose.

A Pipe Badly Dented: How Remedied

If a pipe has been badly dented, it will cause the tone to tremble.

The reason why this oval shape in the middle of the pipe will cause it to tremble is, that the space in the pipe has been diminished. This can be remedied by making a round hole in two blocks of wood, a little larger than the diameter of the pipe; this hole must be lined with felt; by beginning at the top of the pipe and carefully squeezing it with the blocks, from the top down, the dent will be removed, and the speech of the pipe restored. In repairing a zinc pipe, the metal will have to be heated, as zinc is of much the same nature as brass; when heated it becomes flexible.

Wind Causing Pipe to Tremble

If the wind does not strike the upper lip steadily it will sometimes cause the pipe to tremble. This can be remedied by placing a few toothpicks in the wind-way, the toothpicks thus placed will steady or reflect the wind against the upper lip. This is a useful remedy in flute, also in stopped pipes, where the mouth has been cut too high thus causing the pipe to sound its octave harmonic.

To Change the Speech of Pipes

A pipe is sometimes made to speak more softly by pressing the upper and lower lips closer to the languid, which reduces the width of the wind-way. The power of the speech can sometimes be increased by moving the lips in the opposite direction.

Nicking or changing the position of the lips, or the size of the hole in the toe of the pipe, augments or diminishes the intensity of the tone and modifies its quality.

Pipe Speaking its Octave

Sometimes a pipe will sound its octave; all pipes slow of speech are liable to do this such as the Dulciana and Gamba. This may be caused in several ways; dust may have fallen into the wind-way; the pipe may have too much wind; change of temperature may produce the same result; the bellows may not give an equal pressure; or the pipe may have too broad a wind-way, or too high a mouth.

Pipes Changed by Atmospheric Causes

Wooden pipes are subject to a great deal of change by atmospheric causes; in damp weather by the closing of the pores of the wood, making it more firm and sound, which improves the tone; although in very wet weather it is possible for a pipe to swell so much that the height of its mouth will be lessened, and also the width of the wind-way. This would flatten the pitch of the pipe, as well as affect its speech. The opposite is true in a very dry atmosphere. These changes are most noticeable in the large open pedal pipes.

Sometimes in a dry atmosphere, the stopper of a stopped pipe, will shrink and fall into the pipe, raising the pitch and destroying its quality. This can be remedied by putting a thin leather covering on the stopper, but not thick enough to split the pipe, as that would destroy the speech. A stopper should always be driven in perfectly level, in order not to change the tone. Any of the above conditions affect the intonation of the pipe.

The Most Common Faults in the Speech of Pipes

Slowness of speech may be caused by the languid being too high, the upper lip too hollow, the mouth over cut, or the lower lip too bulging. The languid may be lowered by laying the flat part of the lifter on the languid, and gently tapping it, or in the case of a small pipe, by pressure only. The upper lip may be brought out with the lifter. If the mouth is over cut, and the pitch of the pipe will allow, the body must be removed from the foot, and lowered as required, or a new pipe must be furnished. If the lower lip bulges, press it in with the lifter.

Quality of Tone: How Produced

An arched mouth gives a smoother tone than a straight one.

Large scale pipes give a dull fluty tone, and if sustained with heavy wind pressure, a loud tone. A small scale gives a keen, stringy tone. A large mouth gives a dull tone, a small mouth a sharp tone.

The upper lip bent out gives a fluty tone; the upper lip bent in, a sharp tone. The languid high gives a sharp tone. The languid low gives a dull tone. If the wind is directed in the mouth it will produce a fluty tone; if directed in front of it, a stringy tone. A large supply of wind and increased pressure, will produce a sharp and loud tone. A small supply and light pressure, a dull and soft tone.

Overblowing, or Speaking the Octave

Sometimes the languid is too low and should be raised at each corner with the lifter. The wind-hole may be too large; in this case if the mouth is high enough, the wind-hole may be reduced, with the knocking up cup. If the mouth is too low, it may be cut higher, but this must be done cautiously. The upper lip may be out too far, and may be depressed with the lifter; or the lower lip may be in too far, and should be brought out in the same manner.

A Scraping Noise: How Remedied

A scraping noise is sometimes heard with the tone, this may be remedied by slightly increasing the depth of the nicks.

A Windy or Breathy Tone

If the wind-chest and conveyance are sound and a windy or breathy tone is given, the fault must be in the pipe. It is usually a sign of poor making or bad voicing. This may be caused in four ways; the nicks may be too deep, especially in the lip, or too big a wind-way. The mouth may be disarranged, or the pipe foot too short.

In the case of an eight foot pipe, the foot ought not to be less than twelve inches long. Hollowness of tone, is usually caused by over-cutting, or the upper lip is out too far, (see overblowing).

Position of the Lips and Languid

The upper and lower lips must be in an exact line with each other, also in line with the languid. The languid must be in line with the lower lip, and one side must not be higher than the other. The lower lip must maintain the angle given it by the burnisher and not scoop out. The languid must not be too high or too low.

How to Raise the Languid

The languid can be raised by passing a piece of wire from one-sixteenth to one-quarter of an inch in diameter, and about eighteen inches long, up through the pipe foot hole; this wire must be smooth at the ends.

Pipes Refuse to Speak

If a pipe refuses to speak and the mouth and wind-way are free from dust, hold the finger in front of the mouth; if the wind goes out too far to strike the upper lip, the finger will reflect the wind against the lip; or test by gently blowing in the mouth of the pipe, which will reflect the wind and the pipe will speak. It is remedied by bringing out the upper lip a trifle, or by carefully raising or lowering the languid, to give the required effect.

The Pitch of Organs

Organs built some years ago were tuned to high concert pitch, A 453. C 540 concert pitch was not uniform. In some instances the pitch for military bands was as high as A 464. At the present date organs are tuned to international (or French Normal Diapason) A 435, C 517.3; philharmonic pitch (or English Society of Arts) A 440, C 528.

Temperature at which to Tune

The organ should be tuned at a temperature of from 65 to 75 degrees F. In tuning, handle the pipes as little as possible, as touching them will put them out of tune. This is caused by the extra warmth of the hand. After the octave or principal has been tuned, the next set to tune depends upon its position; those farthest away should be tuned first. This order of procedure will avoid reaching over and disturbing pipes that have already been tuned.

It is impossible to put an organ of any size in perfect tune, but the errors should be as small and few as possible. Soft stops tune better to the Principal; as the tuning progresses, their octaves should be tested and kept smooth. Flutes and Gedäckts should not be used to tune other stops to. In tuning make as little change as possible. The action should be in good regulation and repaired before tuning.

Enemies of the Pipe Organ

The two enemies to the pipe organ are temperature and humidity. Temperature changes the pitch; fifteen or twenty degrees rise changes B nearly into C, and vice versa. If the temperature rises the flue pipes sharpen and the reed pipes flatten. Humidity swells and obstructs the mechanism. These weaknesses of the pipe organ require constant attention.

Temperament

The temperament is set on the octave or principal, as this stop is one octave in pitch above the eight feet stops, and one octave below the two feet stops. It thus occupies an intermediate position. Therefore in tuning the other stops to the octave or principal, the difference in pitch is one octave above and below the temperament stop. Stops that are used for solo work, and accompanying, should have a temperament of their own. The best results are obtained in the following way: tune the small c in unison to the octave or principal; then set the temperament; after doing this, the remaining pipes of the stop are tuned in octaves. The other stops will have to be tuned in unison to the octave. The best effect, however, is obtained by tempering each stop or set of pipes.

This requires a great deal more work than to tune in unison, but the result is much better, as individual stops will be in better tune, and they will also blend as well with each other, as if tuned in unison.

Pitch: How Changed (Pipe Organ)

To change the pitch of the pipe organ from concert to international pitch, move the pipes with the exception of the show pipes up a semitone: this will leave the organ within a few vibrations of low pitch. It will be necessary to furnish a new pipe for the lowest note of each set of pipes.

The Result of Closed Swell

Some organists thoughtlessly leave the organ with the swell closed, this results in changing the temperature of the different divisions of the organ. Because of this fact the tuner should at once open the swell, to allow the temperature to become equalized before tuning.

Flue Pipes: (How Tuned)
(See Figure 4, page 16)

Flue pipes are tuned in various ways; by a coil, a shade, a stopper, a cone, or by the ears.

1. Chimney flute. This pipe is half stopped, and is tuned by its ears: these are especially large. It receives its name from its chimney. To sharpen the pitch, spread or open the ears; to flatten the pitch, close or bring the ears closer together.

2. Octave or Principal. This open pipe is tuned with the tuning cone. Pipes that are tuned with the cones, are those not furnished with large ears, stopper coil, or shade. To sharpen the pitch of the pipe, with a sharp quick blow not too forcible insert the point of the cone in the top of the pipe. To flatten it, close the pipe with the cup shaped part of the cone: in a pipe of this style, if the cone is used with too much force, the body of the pipe will give way under the blow, and this will lower the height of the mouth of the pipe, thereby destroying its tone. Before using the cones it is well to rub them with a greasy cloth; this prevents their sticking to the pipe and lifting it out of place while tuning.

After tuning, wipe the cones with a dry cloth. In testing the pitch of a coned pipe, place very slowly the point of the cone along side the upper edge of the pipe; as the beats increase or decrease the pitch is respectively flat or sharp. Sharpen or flatten as stated above. To tune coned pipes without damaging them, it is necessary to have four different sizes of cones.

3. Open Diapason. This is an open pipe, near the top of which an opening is made; this is turned down in the shape of a coil. Raising or lowering the latter, flattens or sharpens the pitch of the pipe.

Special mention must be made of pipes that are to be tuned that have a coil near the top of the pipe, which is rolled down or up, as the pitch of the pipe may require.

If the pipe is out of tune, then by placing the flattened portion of a screw driver on the top of the coil, and against the body of the pipe the beats will grow faster if the pipe is flat; if they grow slower the pipe is sharp.

To sharpen the pitch of the pipe lower the tuner. To flatten the pitch raise the tuner.

Cutting Down New Pipes

In cutting down to pitch a new pipe, that is tuned by a coil, saw the end of the pipe until it is in unison with the semitone below; then measure the diameter of the pipe. If it is one inch the slot must begin one inch from the top of the pipe; as the slot ought always to begin as much below the top of the pipe, as is the measure of the diameter: always cut the slot down from this point.

4. Melodia. An open wood pipe, tuned by a shade made of lead, which is placed on the back of its top.

Wooden Pipes that are Tuned by a Shade

If a pipe is sharp, lower the shade; if flat, raise the shade.

5. Stopped Diapason. This is tuned by moving the stopper up, to flatten, and down to sharpen the pitch. Pipes closed at the upper end by a stopper are tuned by raising or lowering the stopper.

To change the pitch of the pipe, lower the stopper, to sharpen the pitch; raise the stopper to flatten the pitch. If the stoppers do not fit firmly in the pipes, or are in a crooked position, the tone of the pipe will be weak and poor.

Reed pipes are tuned by the tuning wire, and sometimes by the coil cut in the bell, or by raising or lowering the bell; lower the wire to sharpen, raise the wire to flatten the pitch. In tuning reeds the best effect is obtained by tuning them in unison to the Diapason, from small c to four-lined C'''. Then throw off the Diapason, and tune from small c down to great C, in octaves. Reed pipes should be tuned last. They usually need tuning once a week to be in good condition.

If the reeds are in tune, but are not of even power, they can be voiced by respectively raising or lowering the tuning wire to increase or lessen the power of tone. This is applicable only when other conditions of the reed and pipe are right. For instance, dust collecting in the reed, (See reed pipes silent, page 92) or cobwebs, millers or beetles falling into the tube would prevent voicing or tuning the pipe. Sharpening the reed by the spring softens the tone; sharpening it by the slit at the top of the pipe augments the tone. The above conditions should always be taken into consideration, when tuning or voicing reeds, otherwise when the tuning is finished the pipes will be of uneven voice. If, after a reed has been voiced by use of the tuning wire, the pipe is ont of tune, then finish tuning by the coil at the top of the pipe. If there is no coil cut in the bell of the pipe, the bell can be raised or lowered as required. In extreme cases where a reed is too loud, and will not voice down, it can be remedied by placing across the top of the bell, to the depth of about one inch, a small piece of wood about one half of an inch thick, and tapering in shape like the letter V. This V-shaped piece of wood, if properly made will fit the conical shape of the bell. Doing this flattens the pitch sufficiently to allow lowering the tuning wire, in order to soften the tone. (This piece of wood is technically called a Dutchman.)

Tongues Damaged by Kinks

Tongues that are twisted or kinked cannot be used, as it is impossible to get the desired tone quality under such circumstances.

In order to have reeds speak well they must be absolutely clean, and free from dust. A reed pipe should never be blown into as the moisture of the breath will cause particles of dust to cling to the tongue, thereby destroying its tone.

Curving of Reed Tongues

The tongue of a reed can be curved by fastening it to the reed voicing block, then rubbing it from end to end with the shaft of a screw driver. This will curve it slightly as shown in figure 5, page 20. A straight tongue will not vibrate and one insufficiently curved will rattle and have a weak tone. Too much curve makes it loud and slow of speech. A tongue slightly curved will produce the desired tone. (See page 20, figure 5.)

Tuning of Mixtures

Tuning a mixture of two or more ranks, on the electric or tubular pneumatic organ, is accomplished as follows: To tune the five rank mixture, muffle the four shorter pipes of this stop by placing a small piece of cotton batting in the top of each pipe; thus allowing to sound the longest pipe of this set, which is the fifth in pitch.

This pipe is tuned a perfect fifth to the octave stop. When this has been tuned pure, remove the cotton from the next longest pipe on this key and place it in the pipe of the next key above; the pipe that the cotton has just been removed from is now to be tuned a perfect octave above the octave stop. After this has been tuned pure, remove the cotton from the next longest pipe and place it in the pipe of a semitone above; the pipe that the cotton has just been removed from is the 17 or major third, it is now tuned perfect to the octave stop. The remaining two pipes are tuned in the same manner, as the first three of this set. In some tracker organs that are furnished with a mixture, the slider is so arranged that it can be separated for the different sets of mixture pipes by removing a few small pins at one end of the slider. This is very convenient as it saves muffling the pipes when tuning.

Concussion-bellows, Aneometer and Reed Voicing Block
(See Figure 5, page 20)

1. Wind-trunk. 2. Concussion-bellows. 3. Concussion-bellows spring. 4. Aneometer or wind gauge. This little instrument is used in weighing the wind. If the wind pressure of an organ is desired, pour a small quantity of water in the gauge, then remove one of the pipes and place the socket (5) in the pipe foot hole. The compressed wind rushing up through the socket will displace the water in the glass tube. Twice the displacement of the water gives the number of inches of wind. If the water rises one and one-half inches, the bellows will give a three inch wind; if two inches, a four inch wind. The wind pressure is made stronger by adding more weights to those on the top-board of the bellows.

5. Socket. 6. Reed voicing block. (See

curving of reed tongue page 88; also figure 5, page 20.) 7. Bad curve of tongue. 8. Curve too irregular. 9. Curve good, but exaggerated; it should be slightly curved.

10. Tuning wire. This movable piece of wire passes through a small hole in the block. The lower part of the wire is bent in order to press firmly against the tongue, as shown in the illustration.

The portion that vibrates is below the tuning wire, and can be lengthened or shortened as required, to put the pipe in exact tune.

The upper end of the wire is also bent, in order that it may be easily moved up or down: raising it flattens, and lowering it sharpens the pitch.

11. The Reed. This is a small brass tube closed at the lower end. The upper end is slightly smaller than the lower end, to make that part of the reed set tightly in the large hole of the block.

The reed has an opening on the top running lengthwise. Through this opening the wind enters the pipe when the tongue is in vibration.

Reeds Covered with Leather

Sometimes the portion of the reed that the tongue rests on is covered with leather, this is to soften the tone of the pipes.

12. The tongue is a flat, thin, elastic piece of tempered brass, slightly curved. When in position the tongue rests over the

opening just mentioned, with a slight space between the tongue and reed.

13. The Wedge. The wedge is a small piece of wood or brass, driven into that portion of the hole in the block not occupied by the reed and tongue. Its purpose is to hold firmly in position the upper end of the tongue, on which it rests.

14. The Boot. The boot is a metal case, somewhat resembling the foot of a flue pipe. Through this the air passes up to the tongue; the latter being slightly curved when in a state of rest, leaves the opening in the reed free for the passage of air. The air rushing through this opening draws or forces the tongue with it, thus causing it to strike against the reed. The opening now being closed the air cannot pass into the reed until the tongue returns to its former position, which it does instantly. This periodical motion of the tongue, sets the air in vibration thus producing a sound.

15. Tuning Cones.

Reed Pipes Rattle

When the tongue is too close to the reed, curve the tongue slightly. When the wedge is loose, tighten it by driving the wedge in with the shaft of the screw driver. When the tuning wire touches the boot, place a piece of felt between wire and boot. When the tuning coil has been cut too low, and loose edges touch, place a piece of sheep-skin between coil and pipe where they touch.

When the pipes rest against each other, separate the pipes and secure them to the rail with cord furnished for that purpose.

Reed Pipes Silent

Frequently reed pipes will not speak; this is usually caused by a particle of dust having lodged between the tongue and the reed, which may be remedied by taking a piece of paper with a clean edge (such as writing paper) and carefully drawing the paper sideways between the tongue and the reed, which will remove the obstruction. The best remedy for this fault is to take out the wedge and remove the tongue, which allows wiping both the tongue and the reed with a piece of chamois; thus insuring prompt speech and good quality of tone.

The Principle of Pneumatics

The pneumatic action is used to overcome the resistance of the pallets; the motive power being compressed air. The motor is a bellows or diaphragm, always more than twice the size of the pallet.

The Pneumatic Lever

The pneumatic lever is only used for large tracker organs. This contrivance is shown in figure 8, page 93.

There are: 1. The lever or motor, which when inflated lowers the pallet tracker 2. The key tracker, 3, is used only to open the small pallet, 4, and close the escape valves, 6. The spring on pallet, 4,

Fig. 8

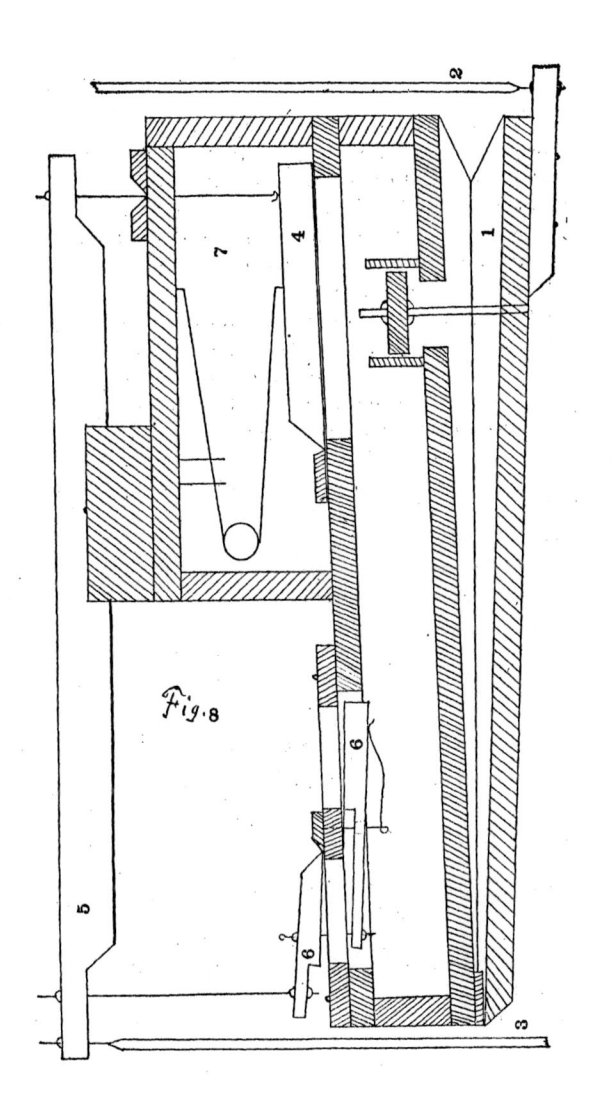

is strong enough to return the key when the finger is removed, and the spring on valve 6 is sufficient to close the valve. The motor 1, in different organs varies in size from two to four inches in width: this is governed by the pressure of wind and size of pallet it must open.

The motors being wider than the spacing of the trackers and pull-downs, it is necessary to arrange them in tiers of five; this allows the connection of the trackers and pull-downs with their respective motors and pallets, to be in direct line with each other.

When a key which is connected with the front end of a back-fall is lowered it pulls down the tracker 3, which lowers the front end of back-fall 5. This opens the pallet 4, in wind-chest 7, and admits wind to the motor 1, at the same time the escape valve 6, closes; this in turn lowers tracker 2, which operates the pallet, thus causing the pipe to sound.

Tubular Pneumatic Action

The tubular pneumatic action is an appliance having small lead, brass or steel tubes or pipes, about three-eighths of an inch in diameter, and as many feet long as are required to reach from the wind-chest to the console. These tubes take the place of back-falls, stickers, squares and trackers. When a key is lowered, it opens the end of the tube directly back of the tail of the key; this is accomplished in two ways, either by a double-seated or puppet-valve, or by a small straight valve covered with sheep-skin on one side.

This action was invented in order to lighten the touch. With this system the key only opens a valve one-fifth the size of the valve in the large wind-chest. It is supposed that Mr. Barker, an organ builder of Bath, England, first introduced pneumatics, as he applied this system to the York Cathedral organ in 1833; the next organ furnished with pneumatic action was that of the Church of St. Denis, in Paris; since that time great improvements have been made. The first use of the pneumatic action in America, was about 1864. A tubular pneumatic action was put in the organ of one of the churches of Manchester, Connecticut, in 1891.

It is by opening and closing of the above valve, that the pneumatic is exhausted and filled again. This takes place as follows: The primary pneumatic exhausts through the tube which collapses the primary pneumatic. The primary pneumatic will then exhaust the secondary pneumatic, while the secondary pneumatic in collapsing opens the pallet or valve, thus allowing the compressed wind to make its way up to the pipe, and cause it to speak. A tubular pneumatic action is apt to be slow in speech.

Tubular Pneumatic Key Action

In this action a thin skin is used to operate the puppet-valve. The tube conducts air to the chamber. This chamber is covered with a piece of thin skin. When the chamber is filled the air lifts the skin and raises the puppet-valve, thus closing the opening at the top of the double-seated valve and opening it at the bottom. This allows the pneumatic to exhaust, and the air in and around the pneumatic, will cause the latter to collapse, and this in turn opens the pallet.

Tubular Pneumatic Stop Action

If the tubular pneumatic stop action comes on or shuts off slowly, test it by beginning at the exhaust directly back of the stop rod. If this opens and closes freely, the trouble is farther back in the organ. If this does not act freely the trouble is in the adjustment of the spring, or the valve may not set properly. If there is a composition board, then test the pnematic, and bearings of the rod, where the combinations are changed. These bearings are liable to be too tight where they pass through the bushing. If this proves all right, next test the pneumatic and the spring at wind-chest. If the spring is too stiff the pneumatic cannot collapse, if it is too weak the pneumatic cannot inflate.

Tubular Pneumatic Inflate Action
(See Figure 7, page 37)

Here we have, 7. Key; 8. Sticker.

9. Exhaust Valve. When the key is lowered, the sticker closes the lower valve,

and opens the upper one. The upper chest being filled with compressed air a portion of the air rushes down into wind-chest 10, and makes its way up the tube 11, to the pneumatic 12; thus inflating the pneumatic, which by means of the tracker wire pulls down or opens the pallet 14. By so doing, the compressed air in wind-chest 13, rushes up into the pipe and causes it to speak. (The chamber 10, as represented in the cut is

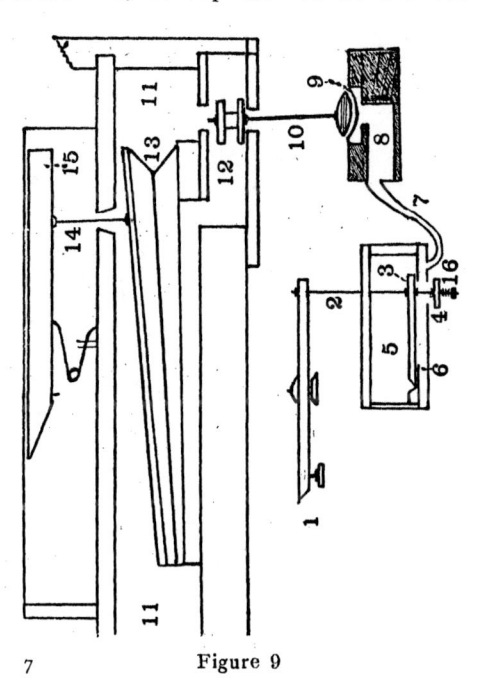

Figure 9

much too large.) As soon as the key is released the lower exhaust valve 9 opens and the top one closes. This allows the air in the chest 10, to escape through the opening caused by the lower exhaust valve. The air now exhausting from pneumatic 12, through tube 11, the pallet 14 aided by the pallet spring and compressed air in chest 13, by means of the tracker wire will close pneumatic 12, thus shutting off the wind from the pipe.

Tubular Pneumatic Inflate Action
(See Figure 9, page 98)

1. Key. When the key is lowered it raises tracker 2; this in turn opens the inflate valve 3, and closes the exhaust valve 4, thus allowing the compressed air from chest 5, to pass into the tube 7, and make its way up the inflate and exhaust tube. This it does in the form of a puff of air, which forces the air in chest 8, against the diaphragm 9, thereby lifting it and carrying the puppet-valve 10, with it. The puppet-valve now being in a raised position the upper portion of the valve closes the opening to chest 11, and uncovers the opening of chest 12. This opening now being uncovered the wind in chest 12, and pneumatic 13, escapes or exhausts, through the opening as stated above. The compressed wind in chest 11, will now cause pneumatic 13 to collapse and lower the upper portion of the pneumatic, to which is attached the tracker 14. This in

turn opens the pallet 15, and allows the air in chest 14 to make its way up to the pipe, and cause it to sound.

16. Spiral spring. The motion of the key 1, being greater than that of the exhaust valve 4, it is evident that the valve will be seated before the key is down, and therefore it is necessary for the tracker to work freely in the valve, in order not to damage the valve on tracker. To prevent the valve from slipping down the tracker, it is furnished with a spring as above stated. When the key is released the reverse of the above takes place, and the pipe ceases to sound.

Tubular Pneumatic Inflate Action
(See Figure 10, page 100)

1. Console. 2. Key. In depressing the front end of the key, the back end rises, drawing with it the tracker 3, and the upper end of the tracker is fastened to the key, with a leather nut or button.

4. Primary valve spring. Its use is to close the valve when the key is released.

5. Wind-chest. 6. Primary valve. On the upper side of the valve is placed a small screw eye, to which is fastened the lower end of the tracker 3. When the tracker is raised as above stated, the valve 6 is opened; this in turn, by means of a wire closes the puppet-valve 7. The opening of the lower end of groove (the groove is at the extreme left end of the tube 8,) now being closed, and the upper end open, a portion of the air in the wind chest 5 makes its way down into

Figure 10

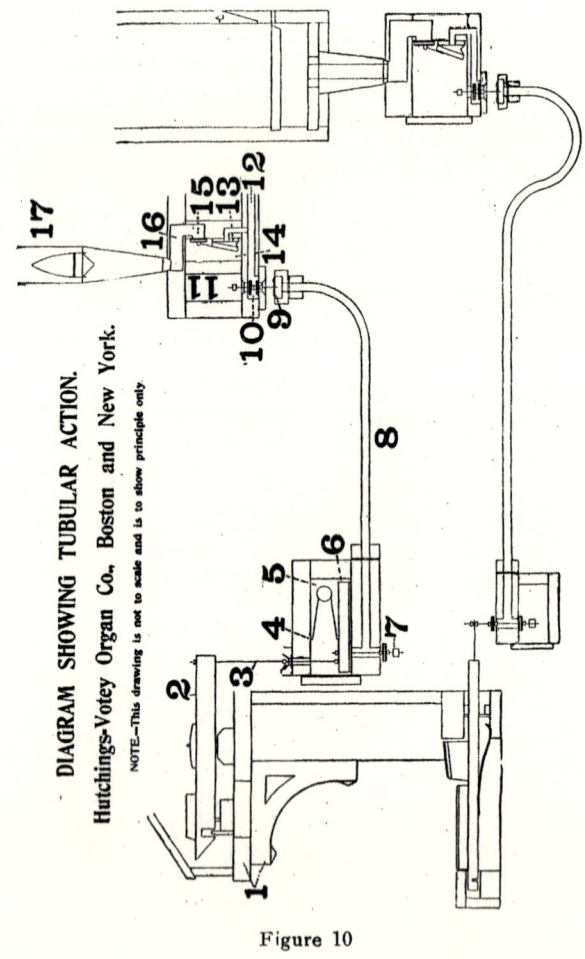

the tube 8, through which it passes up to the diaphragm 9, thus inflating the diaphragm. The diaphragm being connected with the puppet-valve 10, by means of an upright wire, raises the puppet-valve 10, and uncovers the opening on the bottom of the groove 12, and at the same time closes the opening at the upper side of the groove, thus shutting off the passage of wind from the chest 11 to the groove.

The lower end of the groove now being uncovered, a puff of wind that is in the pneumatic 13, can make its escape through this opening in groove 12, that the puppet-valve has uncovered. This allows the pneumatic 13, to exhaust through the groove 12; the compressed air in the chest 14, will collapse the pneumatic 13, which in turn opens the pallet, or valve 15, and allows the compressed air to make its way through the groove 16, up to the pipe 17, and cause it to speak.

The pedal organ is operated in the same manner as the Great Organ. On the extreme end of the pedal is fastened a spring. This spring closes the exhaust, and at the same time opens the lower puppet-valve thus allowing the wind to make its way from the chest, through the tube to the diaphragm, and inflate it. This inflation opens the exhaust and closes the opening to the chest above. The compressed wind in the chest can now collapse the pneumatic. As the pneumatic collapses, it opens the pallet or valve to the pipe, and a sound is produced. When the pedal is released, the reverse of the above takes place, and the pipe ceases to speak.

Tubular Pneumatic Action

Keys will not sound:

When the exhaust valve at the key end of the exhaust tube does not open. See that connections between the stop rod and exhaust valve are not broken, or displaced or out of adjustment.

When the exhaust tube has been damaged. Accidently stepping on the tube, or a heavy weight falling on it, or an abrupt kink in the tube will close the tube, thereby preventing its exhausting the primary pneumatic.

When the primary or secondary pneumatic spring is too stiff, thus preventing the pneumatic from collapsing. This necessitates weakening the spring enough to allow the pneumatic to work.

When the bleed hole in the primary pneumatic is too large.

When any foreign substance has dropped through the sound board and has lodged between the valve of the pneumatic and face of the wind-chest.

When the sheep-skin on the pallet or valve has become unglued and clings to the groove leading to the pipe.

When the sheep-skin on the puppet-valve has warped.

When the leather that forms the walls of the pneumatic has become stiff and hard; in which case the above defective parts should be releathered.

When the pallet is partially unglued from the pneumatic or diaphragm lever, thus preventing them from opening the pallet. In regluing the pallet, be careful that the pallet entirely covers the pallet hole, or it will result in a ciphering.

Keys Cipher

When the exhaust valve at key end of the exhaust tube does not close. This is usually caused by the valve being displaced, or the connections between the stop rod and valve are too tight, or the spring too weak. Properly adjust the above. When the exhaust tube has been punctured or broken, caused by some sharp instrument falling on the tube, or by the tube breaking in passing around corners; either of these faults can be remedied by winding electric tape around the tube where it is broken.

When the screws that hold the frame or rail, in which the end of the exhaust tube is cemented, are loose, thus allowing a leakage of air. Tighten the screws.

When the spring of the primary or secondary pneumatic is too weak, broken or displaced.

When the leather that covers the pallet has warped, thus preventing the pallet from closing.

When there is anything wedged between the pallet and sound board.

When the screws in the top boards, also the bottom boards, of the wind-chest are loose. In this case a number of the pipes will speak.

When the pallet does not seat, or is partially unglued and hangs down, thus uncovering the channel leading to the pipe.

Inflate Action Tubular Pneumatic
KEY AND PEDAL SPEAKING
(See Figure 22, page 105)

1. *Diaphragm Chest.* Containing compressed air. When the pedal is lowered, it removes the valve from the diaphragm, and this allows a portion of the air to pass into the tube.

2. *Diaphragm Chest.* When the pedal bourdon stop is in, this chest is filled with compressed air. The pressure of the air in the chest forces the arched line or diaphragm down against the block. This prevents the air that has entered the tube through the chest 1, from passing the block unless the air-pressure in chest 2 is released. By drawing the pedal stop the air-pressure in this chest is free to external air, thus establishing a continuous channel constituting the normal windway from the diaphragm chest to the primary valve of the pedal organ wind-chest.

3. *Diaphragm Chest. Great to Pedal Organ.* When the coupler stop is in, then the normal windway from the great to pedal organ is closed by the pressure of wind on

Fig. 22

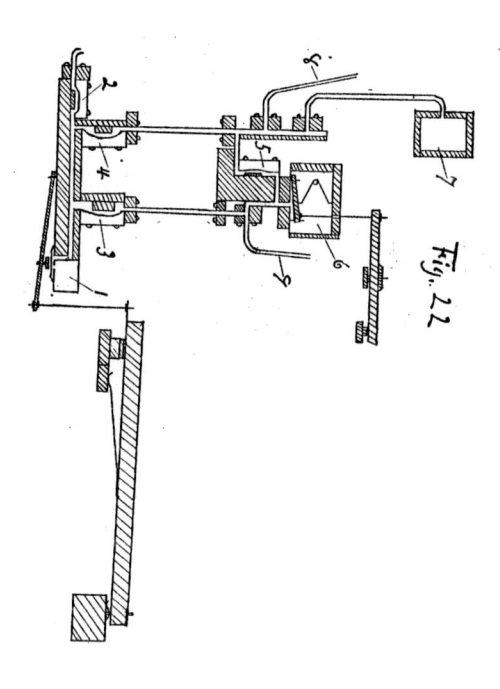

Fig. 23

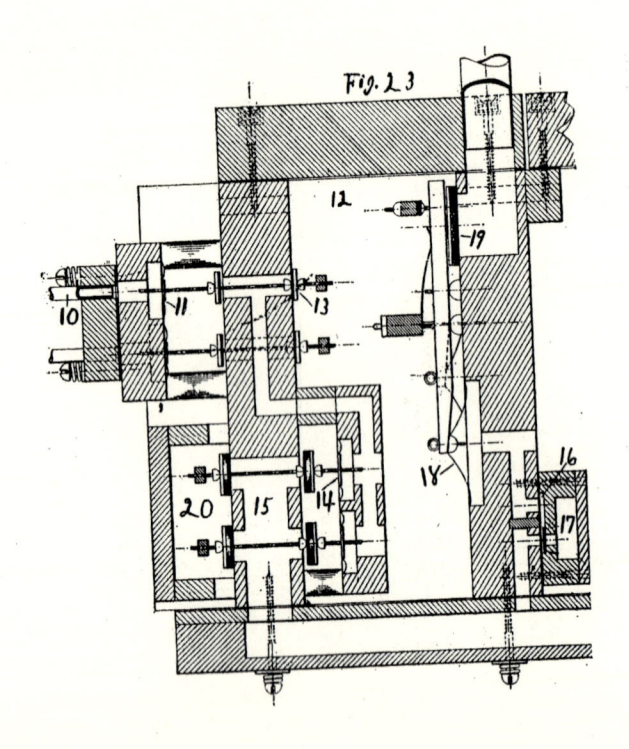

the diaphragm. When the stop-great to pedal is out, then the air-pressure is shut off from this chest, and is open to external air. The branch channel now being open, the air can pass up into the normal windway of the great organ and by so doing the key on the great organ is made to sound with the pedal.

    4. *Swell to Pedal Coupler.*
    5. *Swell to Great Coupler.*

Numbers 4 and 5 are operated in the same manner as number 3.

    6. *Great Organ Key Wind-chest.* This chest contains compressed air. When the key is lowered a portion of the air enters the tube or normal windway and passes to the primary diaphragm of the pipe chest.

    7. *Swell Organ Key Wind-chest.* The air in this chest is operated the same as number 6.

    8. *Normal Windway,* or tube to the primary of swell organ.

    9. *Normal Windway,* or tube to primary diaphragm numbered 11.

The diagram from number 10 to 20 represents the pipe silent. (See fig. 23, page 106)

    10. *Tube* leading to primary diaphragm.
    11. *Primary Diaphragm.* When air-pressure is admitted into the tube 10, it inflates the diaphragm. This moves the spindle to which is attached the diaphragm and the puppet valves. The motion of the spindle closes the puppet valve 13 on the left to external air, and opens it on the right to compressed air.

12. *Wind-chest.* This chest supplies the pipes with air.

13. *Primary Puppet Valve.* When this valve is open, compressed air enters the channel leading to the secondary diaphragm 14, which inflates the diaphragm, and thereby closing the puppet valve on the right. This excludes the air-pressure and at the same instant opens the valve on the left to external air 20.

14. *Secondary Diaphragm.* Its use is to operate the puppet valves.

15. *Normal Windway*, or channel leading to pitman valve 16.

16. *Pitman Valve.* This valve serves to admit and exclude the air-pressure from the pallet diaphragm 18.

17. *Pitman Valve Chest.* When the stop is in, this chest is filled with compressed air and the pitman valve is in a closed position, as shown by number 16. If, however, the stop is out, then the windway of chest 17 is open to outer air and the pitman valve is in an open position, as indicated at the lower end of the groove. The air-pressure of diaphragm 18 can now escape through the groove 15 to the external air, 20. The compressed air in the chest 12 will now collapse diaphragm 18, and at the same instant open the pallet 19; allowing the air to pass up to the pipe and make it speak.

18. *Pallet Diaphragm.* Its use is to operate the pallet.

19. *Pallet.* Its use is to make the pipe

speak and cease speaking.

20. *External Air Chamber.*

The Electric Action

In lowering a key, the tail of the key lifts the key contact which connects with the contact spring. The circuit now being closed, or completed, the magnet lifts the armature, thereby uncovering the bleed, or exhaust, to the primary pneumatic, which allows the pneumatic to exhaust or collapse. This primary pneumatic, in turn exhausts the secondary pneumatic; the secondary pneumatic in exhausting, opens the pallet to the pipe, and thus the pipe is made to speak.

Advantages of the Electric Action

The electric action has some advantages over the tubular as it permits the use of a movable console. Different divisions of the organ can be placed at any distance from the main organ and such distribution has the advantage of making the tone musically effective; the coupling device is unlimited as regards distance.

At a distance of 165 feet electricity is three times quicker in repetition than air in a tube of the pneumatic organ. Conveying the air through a conductor 60 feet long causes a loss of one-fourth of the wind pressure.

Electro Pneumatic Action
(Figure 11, page 110)

The operation of the key action by electricity is not of recent date, as electric

Fig. 11

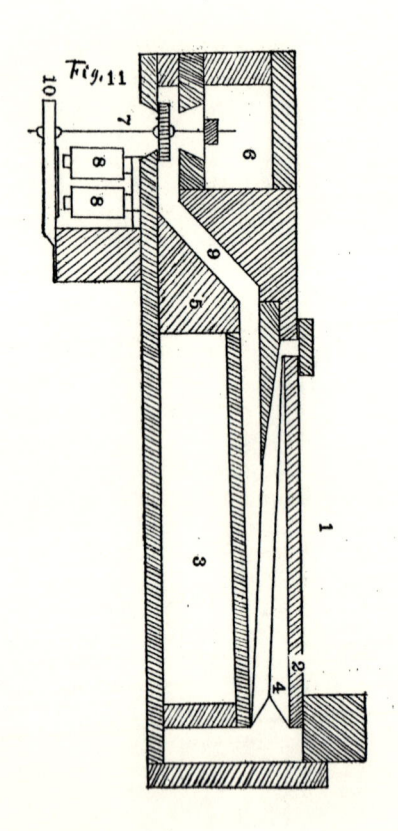

actions were patented in 1852. The cut on the opposite page illustrates one of the early appliances. In this we have:
1. The groove. 2. The pallet. 3. The wind-chest.

4-2. The pneumatic, which takes the place of the pallet in the tracker organ. The pneumatic exhausts through tube 9. This it does only when the puppet-valve 7, is raised by the electro-magnet 8.

The magnet 8, when excited draws up the armature that is attached to the tail of valve 10. When this valve is raised, it uncovers the exhaust tube 9, thus allowing the pneumatic to exhaust, instantly No. 2 which will fall of its own weight and allow the compressed air in chest 3 to pass up to the pipe.

5. Wind-bar. 6. Is a chamber filled with compressed air. The use of this wind is to refill pneumatic 4, when valve 10 has been released.

Electric Action Hutchings Votey Organ Co.
(Figure 12, page 112)

1. Key. When front end of key is lowered the back end of key rises, in which is fastened the key contact 2. This motion of the key causes 2 to come in contact with the contact spring 3; the circuit now being closed, the electric current can pass through wire 4, to magnet 5, and back to the battery 18, and as the circuit is now closed, the magnet will attract the armature 6, thereby

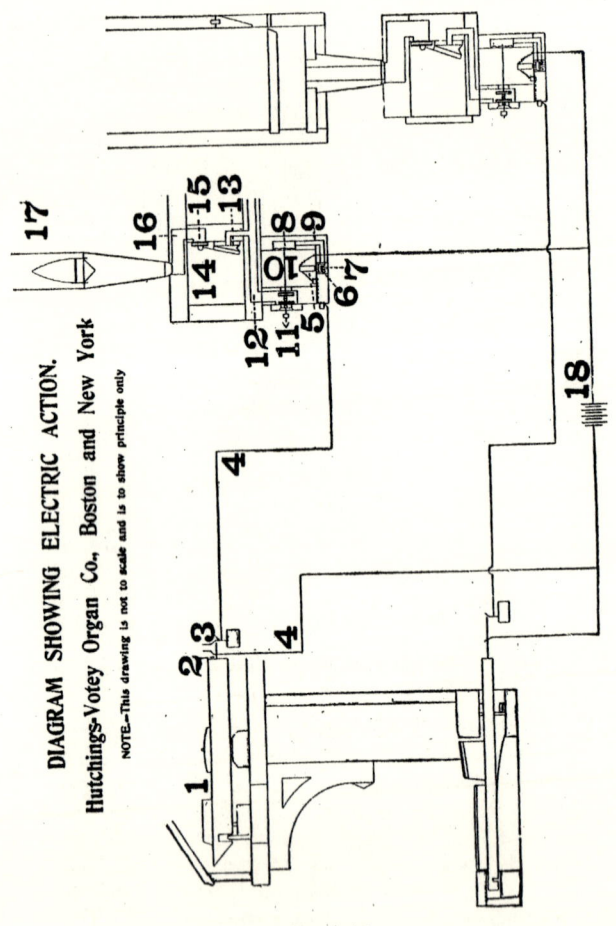

Figure 12

lifting it and uncovering the exhaust hole 7. The exhaust hole now being open, the air can pass from back of the diaphragm 8, through groove 9, and make its escape through exhaust hole 7. With the above condtions the compressed wind in the chest 10 will force the diaphragm 8 toward the groove 9. Owing to the fact that the diaphragm is connected with the puppet-valve 11, by means of a piece of stiff wire, this motion of diaphragm will result in closing the opening between chest 10 and groove 12, and at the same instant open the exhaust to the pneumatic 13, through the above mentioned groove 12, and make its way through the opening uncovered by puppet-valve 11.

The compressed air in chest 14 can now collapse the pneumatic 13, and by so doing open the pallet 15. The pallet or valve now being open, the air can make its way through groove 16, up to pipe 17, and cause it to speak.

18. Battery. The pedal in this organ is made to speak in the same manner as for the Great organ. In lowering the pedal the circuit is closed, at which the magnet lifts the armature, thereby uncovering the bleed hole, thus allowing the diaphragm to operate the puppet-valve; and thereby closing the supply and opening the exhaust of the pneumatic, which in turn opens the pallet, and allows the wind to rush up to the pipe, and produces a sound.

Fig. 13

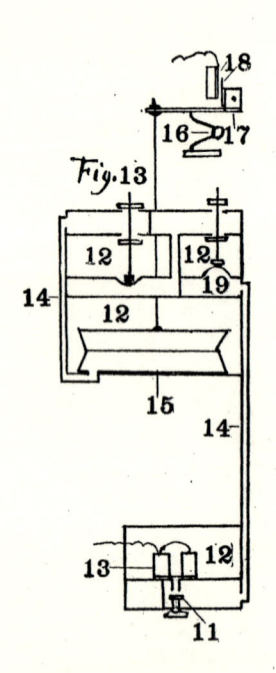

On releasing the pedal, the above conditions are reversed, and the pipe ceases to speak.

In electric organs there may be any number of couplers; as the coupling is done by electric contact.

To Couple Octaves

One end of a wire is fastened to the key wire of the octave note, the other end of the wire is connected to the coupler contact, an octave below. When the coupler stop is out, it places this coupler contact (which is fastened to a roller or blind, that is controlled by the stop) in such a position, that the key contact may touch, or reach the coupler contact; the circuit now being closed, the octave is made to sound.

Section of Electric Coupler Action
(See Figure 13, page 114)

11. Armature. When the circuit is closed by lowering a key the electric current excites the magnet 13 which lifts or attracts the armature, thereby uncovering the hole that the armature rests on and closing the one directly above it. This allows the air in chamber 19 to exhaust through tube 14 and make its way out through the opening caused by lifting of armature. The compressed wind in chest 12 directly above 19 will now force the arched line or diaphragm down into chamber 19 which lowers the puppet-valve, thereby opening the lower valve and closing the upper one: the compressed

wind in chest 12 can now pass up through the opening thus made and make its way down into chamber opposite 19 which will lift the diaphragm that is in a sagged position, thereby raising the puppet-valve and closing the opening on the under side and opening it on the upper side of the chest, thus allowing the air that is in the pneumatic 15 to make its escape through the tube 14 and pass out through the opening on the upper side of the chest. The air in the pneumatic 15 now being exhausted, the compressed wind in the chest 12 will collapse the pneumatic, and by so doing lower the arm that is connected to the coupler roller or the blind 17 which in turn causes the coupler contacts 18 to touch each other; the circuit now being closed the key will cause any pipe or number of pipes to speak that the coupler is designed for.

12. Wind-chests. These chests contain compressed air. 13. Magnet. 14. Exhaust tubes. 15. Pneumatic. 16. Pneumatic spring. Its use is to return the pneumatic. 17. Coupler roller. 18. Coupler contacts. 19. Diaphragm chamber.

Electric Actions Contacts

When contacts of brass, or common metal are used, the action is not absolutely reliable. The best metals for this purpose are gold and platinum. These metals on account of their resistance to oxidization are well suited for this work.

Another very important feature in regard to the reliability of the action, is the rub or friction contact; as it is impossible for dust to remain on a rubbed surface: thus failure is entirely removed while in the touch contact, dirt will lodge between the contact points, and prevent repetition.

Repetition of Electric Action

The electric action if properly constructed can develop a repetition of from fifty to sixty blows per second.

Movable Console

In electric organs, if desired the console can be made portable.

Electric Action

Keys will not speak:

When touch contact is used, if the space between key contact and contact spring is too great. This is regulated either by bending the spring or turning the screw to reduce the space.

When touch contact is used. If dust has collected on the contact point, or if the contact is corroded, clean the contact.

When rub contact is used and the spring is bent too much to come in contact with key.

When the screws are loose, that hold the wire to the contact spring, also to the magnet plate.

When the insulation or winding of the magnet is poor; if the magnet is weak, the best remedy is a new magnet.

When the covering on the armature is loose; in this case use shellac in replacing the covering instead of glue.

When a plunger is used, if the plunger does not move enough to come in contact with contact spring: raise the plunger, or lower the contact spring a trifle.

When a roller is used, if the roller has not motion enough to touch contact spring: raise the regulating button, or glue a piece of felt onto the button.

When the pneumatic spring is too stiff. For further trouble of the pneumatic, see tubular pneumatic action, page 102.

When dust has accumulated under the plunger spring and the brass plate on which it rests: clean points of bearing.

Keys Cipher

When key and contact springs rest against each other: separate the springs.

When the armature does not drop back on exhaust hole, due to the armature being magnetized: then use new armature.

When dust has accumulated on armature.

When a coupler blind is too low—in this case a number of the keys will speak: raise the screws a trifle that regulate the height of the blind.

Electric Stop Action

When electric stop action is used, if the pipes speak, when the stop is off, the contact wires have slipped by each other. Bend the wires enough to prevent passing each other. These wires are directly back of the stop rod.

Wind-Chest Tracker Organ

In the tracker organ each manual has only one wind-chest.

Individual Wind-Chest

In the tubular pneumatic and the electric organs individual wind-chests are used; or in other words each set of pipes, with the exception of the mixtures, has a chest of its own. In the tracker organ the sliders admit or exclude wind from the pipes. In the tubular pneumatic and electric stop action a valve placed at one end of the wind-chest serves the same purpose as the slider; this valve is operated in the tubular pneumatic action by the exhaust tube, and in the electric stop action by the magnet lifting or attracting the armature.

Pallets; Tracker, Pneumatic and Electric

In the tracker organ one pallet serves to admit wind to all pipes of a particular key on any key board. In organs with the tubular and electric actions each pipe has its own pallet.

Self Players

Self playing attachments are sometimes fitted to the pipe organ. The purpose of this is to make possible the use of the organ when the organist is absent. This attachment is operated by a perforated sheet of paper, which sets a pneumatic action in motion. This in turn acts on the pneumatics of the different stops and pipes. With this arrangement the most difficult compositions can be performed.

Complete and Incomplete Stops

Stops that extend all through the range of the manual, such as Diapason, Dulciana, Octave, Mixture and Trumpet, are whole stops.

Stops that are used for one or more sets, by having their sliders divided in the bass, are half stops.

Stops that do not extend all through the manual, and have not the use of a slider of another set, to finish out the compass, or do not borrow, are incomplete stops.

Borrowed Stops

Borrowed stops are those whose pipes are placed in the Swell or Great, and can also be used in some other division of the organ, as the Pedal.

Stops that do not extend through the entire compass of the manual, such as the Oboe and the Clarionet, but the upper octave of which runs into flue pipes, are short stops.

In the pedal organ, when there is only one octave of pipes, and the pedal board has a range of several octaves, the extra pedals are made to sound by returning to the first pipes, by means of tracker action. These are called repetition stops.

The appliances by which stops are operated by pistons, handles, or pedals, in order to bring the organ more completely under the control of the organist, are called accessory stops.

Stops giving a sound that does not correspond with the key held down, (for example, if the key C is used, the pitch of G or E is produced) are called mutation stops.

Stops that sound two, three or five ranks of pipes to each key are called Compound or Mixture stops.

The number of stops necessary to give support to the congregation of a small church, is from eight to ten stops; for a medium size church fourteen to sixteen stops; and for a large church, from twenty-five to thirty stops.

The Influence of Stops

The Octave or Principal, tends to keep the voices in tune. The Manual, Unison, or Diapasons support the voices. The pedal stops mark the time, and keep them together. The deep, heavy tones produce an effect upon the emotions which is at once impressive and inspiring.

Balancing of Stops

If there are two 8 foot stops, to balance it will require one 4 foot stop.

If there are three 8 foot stops, it will require two 4 foot stops and one 2 foot stop.

If there are five 8 foot stops, they should

be balanced by three 4 foot, and two 2 foot stops.

When there are a greater number of stops used than above mentioned, it will be necessary to use a Mixture of two, three or five ranks of pipes.

Mixture Stops where the Break Occurs

The 12th, or fifth, is a stop of 2 and two-thirds feet in length.

The 15th, or octave, is a stop of two feet in length.

The 17th, or major third, is a stop of one and three-fifths feet in length.

Owing to the fact that the length of pipes of the three or five rank mixture, is less than that of the Octave or Diapason, it is evident that with these short lengths of pipes, it would not be practicable to extend the pitch through to the highest key on the organ without a break. The break usually occurs about the middle of the key-board, on F or F sharp. At this point the pitch will again return to that of the lowest key: this is accomplished by making use of the same length of pipes, as are used in the lower half of the key-board.

Armature

An armature in the pipe organ, is a small metal disc covered with blotting paper, or thin leather, and operated by the magnet. It uncovers an opening, and allows the primary pneumatic to exhaust.

If the covering separates from the armature it can be replaced by the use of shellac, which clings to metal much better than glue.

In organs where the armature rests on a brass shoe eyelet, it is best to use blotting paper to cover the armature, as leather will corrode brass. The cause of this is the presence of chemicals used in tanning.

When leather covered armatures are employed, the eyelets should be made of rubber.

Motor

A pneumatic operating a tracker is called a motor.

How to Test an Organ

An organ, if well built, should stand the following tests:

Ascertain whether the feeders, bellows and wind-trunks, are sufficient to supply full organ. Place the wind-gauge on each chest of the organ and by playing full chords, if the pressure varies to any extent it can be seen, by noticing if the water in the gauge indicates a less pressure than required.

The tuning can be tried by drawing all stops; if the heavier stops draw the weaker out of tune, it can be remedied by tuning the weaker, with the stops out that cause the trouble.

If the larger pipes drop, thereby flatting the pitch of the smaller pipes, it proves that the wind-trunks and chests are inadequate to supply the demand.

In the tracker organ, to test the tightness

of the sliders, put off all stops, place the arm on the key-board and hold down a number of keys; if the leak is bad the pipes will speak with some force.

The stops should be tried separately to see if they speak promptly and properly. All composition pedals, and accessary appliances should work quietly and freely.

If any of the above are faulty, they will decrease the tone and utility of the organ.

The Plan Usually Followed in the Arrangement of the Console

The order of manuals, from the top; Solo, Swell, Great, Choir, Pedal.

The stops are placed as follows:

Left.	Right.
Swell.	Solo.
Pedal.	Great.
Couplers.	Choir.

Parts of the Reed Organ
(Figure 20, page 125)

The parts of the reed organ are: 1. Key. 2. Push-pin. 3. Mute. 4. Reed. 5. Reed valve. 6. Valve spring. 7. Wind-chest. 8. Bellows. 9. Exhaust. 10. Exhaust spring. 11. Bellows spring. 12. Pedal strap. 13. Relief valve.

Construction of the Reed Organ

The construction of the air exhausting portion of the organ is as follows:

The difference between the reed and pipe organ bellows is in its construction. Pipe

Fig. 20

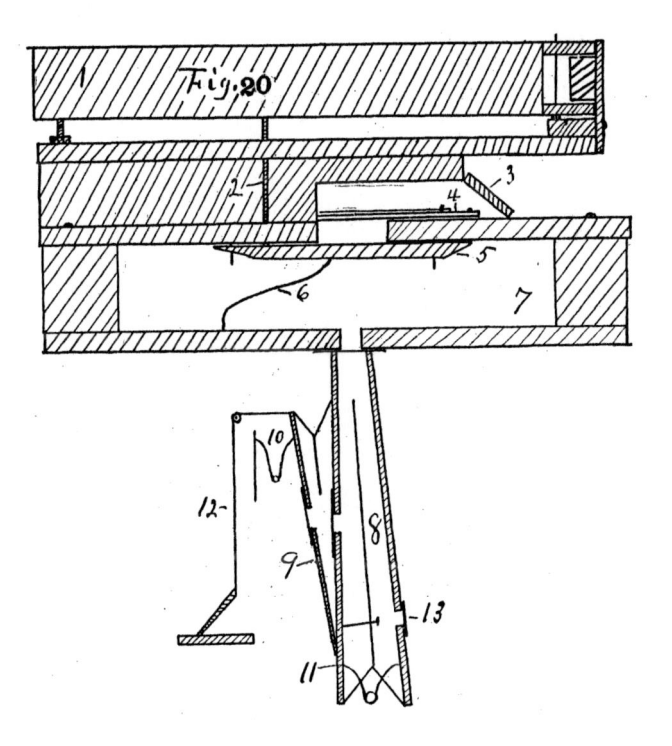

organs have what is termed "the force system;" or, in other words, the air is pumped into the bellows and then subjected to pressure; while in the reed organ the air is pumped out of the bellows or reservoir, which forms a vacuum, and the air rushing in through the reed cells refills it.

This vacuum draws the air through the various channels into the bellows. The bellows used in the reed organ is known as the diagonal bellows, and is wedge-shaped. When the bellows is drawn in or is empty, it has its greatest power. Therefore the greater the exhaust, the slower the vibration of the bass reeds, while the opposite is true of the treble. This accounts for the bass and treble of the reed organ not being in tune when the pressure varies.

The bellows usually has attached to it two springs of 18 pounds pressure each, in order to force the movable board back, when the organ is in use. The force with which the air rushes in to fill the reservoir, depends upon the size and tension of these springs. They are usually made with a pressure of about one and one-half ounces per square inch of surface. The purpose of the bellows, or reservoir, is to maintain an equal pressure or current of air.

The Exhaust

The exhauster is that part of the organ which draws the air out of the bellows. There are always two exhausters, or a double exhaust as it is termed, with a spring of 18 pounds pressure attached to each. The use of the double exhaust is to keep the pressure of the bellows even. They move in opposite directions, one closing while the other opens. The openings in the middle board are technically called "suckers," as it is through these valves that the air is drawn into the exhausters. Those in the exhausters are escape valves. Through these the air escapes after it has been drawn through the reeds, into the bellows as above stated.

The valve on the bellows is called the "relief valve." It is so arranged that the valve comes in contact with a screw placed on the inside of the bellows. This screw opens the valve when the bellows is empty, thus avoiding an undue strain on the bellows and exhausters. These valves are made of sheep-skin, and are hinged at each end or at one side. In the pipe organ the feeder forces the air into the bellows. In the old style reed organ, the bellows was made on the same plan as that of the pipe organ.

Leakage

Defects in the bellows and wind-chest. It is impossible to determine by pumping the organ whether a leak is in the bellows or the wind-chest. If a leak is suspected, it will be known by the rapidity with which the bellows returns to its normal position.

If, after the air has been pumped out of a

bellows, it requires fifteen seconds or more to refill, it is in good condition. If it fills in less time than this, a leak exists. Whether the leak is in the bellows or the wind-chest may be determined by investigating as follows:

    First. Remove the top of the wind-chest. This is done by taking out the screws that pass down through the outer edge of the sound-board.

    Second. Cover the suckers on the bottom board with a piece of paper.

    Third. Pump out the air by means of the exhaust; if the bellows now returns to its normal position in less than the required time, it is apparent that the leak is in the bellows.

Should the bellows not return in less than the required time, it proves that the leak is in the wind-chest. If there is a leak in the organ, it is best first to examine the bellows, as that is the heart of the organ, after which trace up the air passages and valves.

The valves in the reed-organ bellows are placed on the outside of the front board of the exhaust, also on the same side of the back board on the inside of the exhaust. If these valves become disarranged or warped or stiffened by age, or if something in the form of a chip lodges between the valve and the board, or if the valves are badly eaten by mice, the air will rush back into the exhaust as fast as it is pumped out of the bellows. The effect of this on the organ is a weak tone, and the pumping apparatus moves without much resistance.

This same result is also caused by the breaking of either the exhaust or bellows springs. If a bellows spring breaks on the inside, place a new spring on the outside of the bellows. This can be done by fastening a small cleat, or lug of wood, to the back board of the bellows. Let one end of the spring rest against this lug, the other against the frame of the bellows. If the broken spring in the bellows has dropped down to the lower part of the bellows and is not wedged, do not disturb it, as it will do no harm. If, however, it has become wedged and interferes with the action of the bellows, or is liable to make a hole in the rubber, it can be removed by loosening the rubber from the wood at the nearest point to the spring. Loosen just enough to allow the hand to reach in to remove the spring. In replacing the rubber thus loosened, in addition to cementing or gluing it to the board, drive in small tacks a few inches apart.

The Wind-Chest

The wind-chest is a long, shallow, tight box, fastened with screws to the top of the reservoir. A wind-chest is in reality a second reservoir. One of the difficulties connected with the wind-chest is that the bottom board, as well as the top or soundboard, is liable to crack or warp. If the screws that fasten the chest are not furnished with washers, the screw heads will cut into the wood and split it.

How to Remedy These Faults

If the wind-chest is cracked, scrape the shellac from each side of the crack, then fill the crack with cotton which has been saturated with glue. After this has been done, glue a piece of sheep-skin over the crack.

If the rubber of the reservoir or exhaust is cracked or broken, it can be repaired by cementing a piece of rubber over the break. Before putting on a new piece of rubber the surface of the old must be cleaned with benzine, thus insuring the adhesion of the cement. A leakage of air is a serious matter, and should be stopped if possible. Nearly all leaks may be traced by the sound of the air drawing through the crack. If it cannot be detected by the ear, when a lighted candle is held along the walls of the wind-chest the leak will be discovered, as the current of air will draw the flame.

Should the leak be between the top and bottom boards of the wind-chest, due to the stripping of the screw threads, it may be remedied, by gluing a small piece of wood, the shape of a shoe peg, into the screw holes of the bottom board of the chest.

Reeds Ciphering

Reeds speak before the keys are touched:
1. When the valve leaks. This can be tested by drawing out a stop with a soft

tone. Then gently pump and increase the exhaust. If the valve leaks, the reed will begin to speak.

2. When there is something on the valve which will not allow it to close. This can sometimes be removed by taking out the reed, and allowing the air to pass through the reed chamber; if this fails to remove the obstruction, the sound board, or top of the chest, must be taken off.

3. When the valve has warped. Trim it or make a new one.

4. When the sheep-skin that covers the valve has warped. Re-cover it.

5. When the valve spring is weak. Put in a new spring.

6. When the spring is broken or displaced. Put in a new spring.

7. When dampness has loosened the leather. Re-cover with a new piece of leather.

8. When the valve has become caught on the direction pins. This can sometimes be replaced by means of a long needle, passed down through the push pin hole, which carefully works the valve back to its place. Should this fail, the top of the wind-chest must be removed.

9. When the valve binds on the direction pins. Remedy this by adjusting the pins so as to allow the valve sufficient freedom to work.

10. When the mute hinge screws pass through into the reed cell and are not tight.

11. When the push pin binds, either it has become warped, or some hard substance has got into the push pin hole. If warped, take out the pin and smooth the warped portion with sandpaper. In freeing the hole of hard substance, do so cautiously, as there is danger of the obstruction dropping down on the valve, thus causing a ciphering.

12. When the key sticks. The key may bind on to the guide pin. This can be remedied, if the bushing is too tight, by enlarging the puncture. If it binds at the ends of the puncture, or the part not bushed, gauge out the same.

13. When there is pressure on the key from above; which will usually be found around the key rail. This is remedied by placing pieces of felt between the key blocks and the rail.

14. When there is a crack in the reed chamber. Glue pieces of sheep-skin over the crack.

15. When there is no relief valve. For arrangement of the valve see page 125.

16. When the coupler action is too closely adjusted.

17. When the mute is not furnished with an automatic valve, to equalize the pressure of air in and around the cell. This valve is placed at the upper end of the mute, and is arranged to cover and uncover a small hole in the wind-chest. When the mute is closed it opens this valve.

Reeds Sounding the Semitone Above and Below the Note Held Down

If the air is drawn from one cell to the next it will result in sounding the reed of the semitone above or below. This is caused by the separation of the reed cell from the reed or sounding board. To remedy it remove the top of the wind-chest, stand it up on end, take out the valve and reed, and with a small camel's-hair brush fill the crack with shellac from end to end. In using the shellac do not allow any to remain on the portion of the wood where the valve is. Also clean the reed channel before putting back the reed.

Position of Pedal Reeds

Sometimes in pedal organs the reeds are placed in a wind-chest directly over the end of the pedals. To remove the reeds disconnect the pedals. This is done by unclasping a hook or button that holds the pedals to the organ case. The reeds may be taken out of the cells by lifting up the swell mutes of this set.

The Study of Reeds

The reeds used in the reed organ are the free reeds,—the tongue in vibrating passes through the frame instead of striking it. Their tongues are made of rolled brass, or the brass is rolled to temper them. The tongue is fastened to the block or frame in various ways: sometimes with one or two rivets; also by sliding the tongue into a groove; while in some cases the tongue and the block are made of the same piece. The last mentioned is one of the latest devices, and is considered the best, as the tone is smoother and the vibration freer than in the old style reed.

Reeds are composed of three parts,—the reed frame, the tongue, and the rivet. The names are given to the separated parts. The base of the reed frame is called the heel, and the point is called the toe.

How the Tone is Produced

The tone of a reed is produced by the tongue which, when drawn through the block, bounds back, thus causing the air to vibrate by cutting the wind pressure, and allowing it to flow again, by its downward and upward movement, or vibration.

The pitch is governed by the length, size, and number of vibrations of the tongue. Sixteen vibrations of a reed tongue per second is the least number that will give a musical tone.

Small reeds vibrate as many as eight thousand times per second. The tongue always begins to vibrate from above the frame.

The rate of vibration is due:

1. To the air pressure on the tongue. This is governed by the springs on the reservoir.

2. To the length of the tongue; which is

governed by the laws of vibration. The longer the tongue the lower the pitch; the shorter the tongue the higher the pitch.

3. To the elasticity of the metal used in the tongue, which is necessary for a tone.

4. To the weight of the toe as compared with the weight of the heel.

How Reeds are Tuned

Reeds are tuned by filing or scraping the heel to flatten the pitch; and by filing and scraping the toe, to sharpen the pitch.

How to Determine the Pitch of Reeds

The pitch of a vibrating reed is detected either by placing the hand in front of the reed-cell, or by closing the mute. If sharp the beats will become slower, if flat they will become faster.

The above method is for unisons, and can only be used in this way when the reed tested is being tuned. If, however, a reed of the back set is to be tuned to the front, the result of the beating will be the opposite of the above, if tested by placing the hand in front of the cell of the front reed. If sharp, that is if the back reed is sharp, the beats will increase. If flat, they will decrease.

In octave work the pitch is tested by very slowly letting up the key of the reed to be tuned. If sharp, the beating will cease, if flat, it will be accelerated.

How to Test Pitch

The pitch of a reed is always found by applying this test,—Flat, fast, file the toe. Sharp, slow, scrape the heel; or, flat, fast, file,—F. F. F. Sharp, slow, scrape,—S. S. S.

The Size of Reeds

The size of the different sets of reeds in the reed organ depends upon the scale or size of the Diapason or foundation stop; and all others are made with reference to this and run in proportion to it.

Why Reeds Get Out of Order

1. Dust gathers in the cell.
2. A chemical change takes place in the metal of which the tongue is made.
3. A gradual weakening occurs in the recoiling power of the tongue.

New Tongues

In putting in a new tongue it is best to file the tongue as near as possible to the same thickness as the tongue of the reed,—a semitone above or below the one being repaired,—before riveting it to its frame. In filing the tongue, avoid leaving a square nick or shoulder on the surface of the tongue. The surface of the tongue must maintain a gradual concave form from the heel to the center, and from the center to the toe a gradual slant.

How Reed Tongues are Filed

Reed tongues of the high octave are filed thin at the toe, and left thick at the heel, while just the opposite is true of the lower octave. Reed tongues in the bass are sometimes loaded by riveting an extra piece of brass to the toe of the tongue.

A tongue should be filed uniformly (flat on top), and should occupy a central position in the reed frame.

Cleaning the Organ

An organ should not be tuned until after the reeds have been thoroughly cleaned, which will make it very nearly in tune again, as it often happens that the dust, collected on the tongues of the reeds, throws them out of tune with each other. In cleaning the reed organ, take out the key strip, and back of the case.

Wipe the dust from the top of the reed-cell chest and sounding board. Take out the reeds, and place them at one side, being careful not to mix them. Wipe the dust from under the stop mutes, and around the reed cells. Pump the organ with considerable force, and hold down the keys in groups of a half dozen notes each. This will allow sufficient air to pass through the cells to carry all small particles of dust in and around the cells with it.

Cleaning the Reed Tongues

This can be done by using a tooth-brush. Always brush the tongue on the upper and lower surface from heel to toe. If a tongue is absolutely clean, by holding the reed toward the light no dust will be seen around the edges of the tongue. The reed is then ready to be replaced in its cell. Reeds cleaned in this manner will give more tone, and be nearly in tune again. Quite frequently after a reed, which has been taken out and replaced, it will be out of tune, and always flat, if it was in exact tune before being removed. However, after it has been in place a short time it will sharpen again. The reason for this is that the heat of the hand expands the metal of the reed, thereby changing its pitch.

If a reed comes out very hard, before putting it back put a little bees-wax on the edges of the frame.

Rattling Reeds

A reed will sometimes rattle if the reed cell cramps or springs the reed frame against the reed tongue. This will occur only to large reeds when the cell is too small for the reed. To remedy this, file the edges of the reed frame a trifle.

Sometimes the octave coupler is the cause of rattling. This lever is under the keys. To remedy this rattling, take up the keys and tighten the screws where connecting rods are fastened to the lever.

If the mute springs rattle when they are resting lightly on the mute, place felt between the springs and mute.

Tuning the Organ

In tuning the reed organ, make as little change in pitch as possible, for the less the change the longer it will stay in tune. This can be accomplished only by ascertaining at what pitch are the greater number of reeds.

How to Change the Pitch

To change the pitch of the reed organ from concert to international, move the reeds up a semitone. This will leave the organ within a few vibrations of the desired pitch, if it was previously up to high pitch. Changing the pitch in this way necessitates providing a new reed for the lowest note of each set of reeds. If the reed frames are beveled in the upper part of the organ, and if in the lower portion they are square, it will be necessary to bevel the square frame by filing the edges where the break occurs.

Voicing of Reeds

Never under any circumstances should the shape of the tongue be changed, except in voicing. There are four qualities of tone.

1. Organ Tone, as represented by the Melodia, Diapason, and Bourdon.
2. String Tone, as represented by the Violoncello, Gamba, and Violin.
3. Reed Tone, as represented by the Trumpet, Clarinet, and Hautboy.
4. Flute Tone, as represented by the Flute.

Reeds may be varied in the following ways:

By the length of the tongue.
By the thickness of the tongue.
By the width of the tongue.
By the shape of the tongue.
By the shape of the reed cell.

There are two distinct qualities in the voicing of reeds,—character and intensity.

The character of a reed is determined by the shaping of the tongue. The speaking quality of a reed may be determined by the thickness or thinness of the tongue.

A breathy tone is changed by curving the tongue.

The intensity of a tone is affected by the shape of the tongue, and the pressure of the air.

Voicing is giving the reed a certain tone character other than pitch, and is accomplished in three ways. (1) By altering the dimensions of the reed, as regards length, breadth, and thickness. (2) By changing the position of the reed tongue, on the frame, its height or depth above or below the frame, (this will also affect the pitch of the reed, flatting it if the tongue is too high, and sharping it if it is too low. It will also make the tone too loud if the tongue is too high, and too soft if it is too low. (3) By varying the curve of the tongue and the construction of the cell. A reed will not change its character of tone, unless the position of its tongue has been changed.

This can happen by using a dull reed scraper, thereby crowding its tongue down, which will soften the tone. In voicing a set of reeds any curving of the flat position of the tongue will produce a change of tone. A perfectly flat tongue will give a loud tone, and a curve or twist in the tongue will give a soft tone.

Character of Reed Tones

The character of reed tones depends upon the reed dimensions for a given pitch; upon a long slim tongue for a reedy tone; upon a broad and short tongue for a fuller tone; and upon the presence or absence of harmonics.

Celest Reeds

Some organs have what is called a "celest set" of reeds. This set usually begins at one-line C' and extends through the upper part of the organ. It is tuned sharp of the front set, beginning with three beats per second, on one-lined C', and slightly increasing as the pitch sharpens. Sometimes the celest is tuned flat, but the effect is not so brilliant as when tuned sharp.

The celest is simply a set of reeds, tuned "out of tune" with the rest of the organ. In some cases this effect is produced by lowering the mute of this set. Thus there are two ways of producing a celest,—one by tuning, the other by use of the mute.

Tone of Reeds and Position of Mutes

The position of the mute has a great deal to do with the tone of the reeds. It should never be placed in such a position as to allow one end to rise above the other. They should both be alike. The mute is one of the great difficulties to be overcome. It frequently warps and throws the reeds out of tune. It also allows the reeds to speak when the stop is in. To guard against this, the stops should never remain out when the organ is not in use.

Silent Reeds

If a reed refuses to speak, it may be on account of too much air pressure around the sides of the tongue, or the tongue may be too thick and stiff. There may be dust in the reed. If the tongue is too low, raise it by running the blade of a knife under the tongue. If the tongue is too high, it can be lowered by crowding it down with the thumb. A tongue when at rest should be a little above the frame.

Tone Resonance

The resonance of the organ case has a great deal to do with the tone.

Qualifying Tubes

These tubes which are placed over the reed cells are made of metal, and give a decided change in the tone character. They are used simply to give the reeds a more mellow tone, and in tuning one should notice whether there is a tuner on the tube; if so, the reed when only slightly out of tune can be adjusted by the tuner on the tube. The vocalion organs are made on this plan and have a force bellows. These tubes were invented in 1870.

Always examine the mutes and their springs before tuning, as it will often save a great deal of trouble. These springs are apt to break. Sometimes they are made of German silver, but usually of spring brass.

Stops and Speaking Reeds

Reeds speak when keys are lowered. Sometimes a mute will not rest firmly on all reed cells. When this defect exists certain reeds will speak when the stop is in. To remedy this, glue a thin piece of paper, shaped like the small letter "n," on that portion of the cell against which the mute rests. This piece of paper will cause the mute to close the cell and prevent the reeds from speaking.

Reeds will speak when the stop is in, when the rubber that forms the hinge to the mute is cracked. Remedy this by gluing a new piece of rubber onto the mute.

If the mute springs are too weak, if the stop does not close the mute, if the mute is warped, the reeds will speak. This can sometimes be remedied by loosening the sheep-skin and gluing a piece of paper between the skin and the mute, where it is warped.

Automatic Valve to Prevent Ciphering

Some organs have an automatic valve placed under the upper end of the treble mute. This device is to prevent the reeds from ciphering and works as follows: When the mute is closed it opens the valve, which in turn uncovers a hole leading into the wind-chest which allows the air that is between the mute and in the cells to be drawn into the chest. The vacuum in the reed cells is now equal to that in the chest; ciphering is prevented.

Fine dust in an organ will choke the reeds quicker than anything else. If the push pin has been badly eaten by mice, great care should be taken in removing it, in order not to have any of the small splints drop down on the valve.

The Tremulo

The object of the tremulo is to produce a certain beating or wavering of tone. There are two kinds of tremulos in use in the reed organ, one called the fan tremulo, the other the valve tremulo. The fan, or vox-humana, is made so that the air outside of the wind-chest is set in motion, and it is operated by the opening of a valve which allows the air to pass into a small box on the outside of the chest, in which is a little fan wheel; and as the air passes through this box into the wind-chest, it sets in motion the fan on the outside. If the fan sticks, loosen the bearings, as sometimes the shaft of the fan becomes warped.

The valve tremulo is made in such a way that when the stop is drawn the air rushes into the wind-chest, and sets in motion a valve, which by its rapid vibration cuts off the air, thus causing a tremulo. Of the above tremulos the fan is the best. When an organ has a partition in the wind-chest, it is simply to give the tremulo to that part of the organ to which it is attached.

The Action

The dip of the reed organ is a strong three-eighths of an inch. In organs where the octave coupler is used, the action of the coupler is on the collar of the push pin, and it is through this device, with the aid of the coupler action, that the keys couple in octaves. The object of the coupler is to aid the player in using more organ.

Why Keys Stick

1. Something may become wedged between them. 2. The key binder may be too tight. 3. The key may bind on the guide pin. 4. The key slip may be too close to the keys.

The Stop

The reed organ stop, consists of the label, head, rod, and mute.

Pedal Straps

When the pedal straps are broken, the best remedy is new ones. The material used is made especially for this purpose, and may be secured from a tuner's supply company. In cases of emergency, when an organ must be repaired at once, the necessary material, which is a webbing, can be bought at a harness maker's.

How to Put in a New Strap

In some organs the lower front panel can be removed by taking out a few screws. In this style of organ it is an easy matter to put in a new strap. If this panel is not movable, the organ will have to be turned over on its back, to take out the screws that fasten the strap to the exhauster.

Before fastening the strap to the exhaust its end must be passed over the pulley; this pulley is usually fastened on the inside of the lower front panel. After the upper end of the strap has been secured to the exhaust, the lower end is attached to the pedal; in fastening this end of the strap to the pedal, it must be as follows. When the pedal has been lowered as far as the foot would naturally move it, the strap must fully open the exhaust, if this is not so, the full use of the exhaust is not obtained. If the strap is made too short, there will be danger of wrenching the walls of the exhaust, thereby weakening them, and causing the exhaust to leak.

Leveling Keys

In some organs when the top of the windchest must be taken off it is necessary to remove the keys: this is done by loosening the key binder, which is fastened at the tail of the keys with screws; next take out the push pins; put them to one side, as these pins are not all the same length, they must not be mixed; if by accident they should become mixed, they will, when they are replaced, throw the keys out of line. This is remedied by changing the longer pins to the low keys, and the shorter ones to the high. It will be very difficult to level the key-board in this way; it can however be done by the use of new push pin stock, or by taking the pins of the low keys and gluing a piece of paper or postal card on the upper end of the pin, and with a sharp knife trim the paper to the exact size of the pin; unless the keys are very low they can be leveled in this way.

Reed Scraper

In using the reed scraper, if it is put in the cell too far, it will catch on the end of the tongue, and break the tongue.

The Grand Concert Organ

The largest and, as an entirety, the most perfect king of instruments yet built is the Grand Concert Organ, a product of the Los Angeles Art Organ Company for the Louisiana Purchase Exposition. In it are united extraordinary size with consequent volume, successful construction for ease in playing, and approved innovations in the production and distribution of tone.

The magnitude of the organ is well shown by enumerating a few of the specifications.*

It consists of five manuals and pedals. The manuals have sixty-one keys each, and contain one hundred and ten speaking stops, and eight thousand nine hundred and seven (8907) pipes, metal and wood. The key boards are placed as follows: The first or lower is called the Great Organ, the second the Choir Organ, the third the Swell Organ, the fourth the Solo Organ, the fifth the Echo Organ. The Great and Swell Organs have two departments each for the new system of tone production and distribution. The first division of the Great Organ is unexpressive. This division contains all of the foundation stops such as the Open and Double Open Diapason, and Grand and Sub Principal, etc.; thirteen speaking stops in all.

The second division is inclosed in a Swell box, and the folds or blinds are entirely under the control of the Organist. The organ having a portable Console the folds are operated by electricity, which is accomplished in the following manner: The performer in lowering the swell pedal makes an electric contact, and this electric device is furnished with ten contact points which operate a bellows much the shape of a con-

---

*At the expiration of the Exposition it was expected this organ would be placed in its permanent home, Convention Hall, Kansas City, Missouri; but this did not take place, as it is reported the organ is for sale for the sum of $62,000. It cost the Los Angeles firm that built it $82,000.

cussion bellows; this bellows in turn operates the folds to any degree desired from the closed position to that of being fully open. This division contains the stops belonging to the 8 and 16 feet harmonic series; also the important reed stops of the Great Organ. Owing to the flexibility of this division the increased value of its tonal effects are capable of great modification; it is impossible to obtain these results on the old plan of construction. The second division can be used with or without the first division.

A contrivance called double touch has been devised by the Los Angeles Art Organ Company; it is intended to increase the tonal effects and render the expressive division of the greatest value attainable. The contrivance consists of a second contact; and by slightly increasing the pressure on the keys the performer instantly adds the effect of any combination of stops that are drawn in the second division; it can also be brought on or thrown off by thumb pistons. This division comprises 13 speaking stops.

The Choir Organ

The stops in this division are especially adapted for accompanying. The reeds used are the free reeds and the tone is as smooth as that of the flue pipe. This department is inclosed in a swell box and contains 20 stops. The specification of this division shows great variety of tone. It is controlled by its own manual and also by that of the Great organ manual by means of Double Touch.

The Swell Organ

A most complete and unique organ in character and variety of tone! This department is in itself a complete concert organ, capable of interpreting almost any orchestral effect. It contains thirty-four stops and has two thousand eight hundred and sixty-seven pipes; the stops are arranged in two divisions both of which are in swell boxes, and can be used independently or as a unit. The first division contains twenty-three stops and 1586 pipes. The specifications show the orchestral instruments used, as represented by the Flutes, Piccolo, Fagotto, and Contrafagotto, Violin Diapason, Clarinet, Oboe, Corno di Bassetto and Horn. This division can be brought on or thrown off the Swell manual by thumb pistons. The second division of the Swell organ has 11 stops and 1281 pipes; this department of the Swell is to represent the string division of the orchestra, and all of the pipes in this division with the exception of the Contra-Basso and Violoncello are made of pure tin. This division can be brought on or thrown off of the Swell manual by thumb pistons and also by the Double Touch, of the Swell Organ.

Mr. George Ashdown Audsley, F.R.I.B.A. says: "This remarkable subdivision is inclosed in an independent swell box (No. 3), and can be brought on or thrown off the third clavier by thumb pistons; and is also connected with the clavier by the double touch of the Swell Organ. By the unique tonal apportionment and the double expressive powers of this division, the orchestral effects it can alone produce under the hands of the virtuoso will transcend everything hitherto possible on the largest Organ. A book could be written on the countless tonal effects possible on this compound, expressive division alone. It may be interesting to learn that with the thirty-four speaking stops contained in this compound division, no fewer than seventeen billion, one hundred and seventy-nine million, eight hundred and sixty-nine thousand, one hundred and eighty-three (17,179,869,183) distinct tonal and expressive combinations or effects are possible, without resort to octave or sub-octave coupling, or any multiplying device whatever. Some idea can be formed of the number of tonal effects above given when it is calculated if a different combination was drawn every minute, day and night, it would require above thirty-two thousand six hundred years to complete the performance."

The Solo Organ

This organ is placed in a swell box and represents the brass-wind division of the orchestra. It contains 18 stops, some of which are placed on a wind pressure of 7, 10 and 20 inches.

The Echo Organ

It is placed in swell box No. 5, and has 12 stops of delicate intonation. This division, as the name indicates, is placed at some distance from the main organ.

The Pedal Organ

The pedal organ contains 30 stops and 1152 pipes, the largest pedal organ ever built; the range of pitch is from 4 feet to 64 feet, and in volume from that of the Dulciana to the powerful tone of the 32 and 64 feet.

Mr. Audsley further says:

"In addition to the above unique tonal appointment and apportionment, the Organ is provided with thirty-six couplers by means of which the five manual claviers are coupled to the Pedal Organ clavier; and by means of which the five manual claviers are connected together in twenty-five different relations, or, including subdivisions, twenty-eight different relations. There are eight Pedal Organ couplers; eleven manual unison couplers, seven sub-octave couplers, and ten octave couplers—an array of couplers never before approached in any Organ in the world.

"There are five Tremulants acting on the five expressive divisions and subdivisions, exclusive of the expressive subdivision of the Great Organ.

"There is an adjustable Combination System for the entire Organ, commanded by forty-six push buttons located between the manual claviers, and there are ten pedal movements chiefly controlling the vast expressive powers of the instrument—expressive powers that far exceed those of any other Organ in the world.

"The entire Organ is fitted with the Fleming Patent Individual Valve Electro-Pneumatic Action, which for promptness and certainty of operation and durability stands at the head of electro-pneumatic actions.

"The instrument will be played from two independent Consoles of the most perfect construction and design. The most important Console is movable, and is connected to the Organ by an electric cable one hundred and fifty feet long. This Console contains the radiating and concave pedal clavier; the five manual claviers; the one hundred and forty draw stop knobs; the five Tremulant draws, and the thirty-six Coupler draws, the forty-six push buttons belonging to the Adjustable Combination System; and all the foot pedals controlling the expressive powers of the whole Organ, etc., etc. This Console is for the Virtuoso who performs in the usual manner with hands and feet.

"The second Console is stationary, and is entirely devoted to the builders' Patent Double-Roll Automatic Self-Playing Attachment—the only reliable and sufficient self-playing attachment invented for the Pipe Organ. Through the agency of the double or twin rolls, the most complicated orchestral scores can be rendered with absolute accuracy; and compositions can be performed which are far beyond the powers of the most accomplished organist. This Console resembles that first described, except that it does not possess the manual and pedal claviers, which are not necessary where the Double-Roll, Self-Playing Attachment appears. It is difficult and indeed, well nigh impossible, to realize what can be achieved in the world of music through the agency of this wonderful Console. Within its arms, so to speak, sits the musician, entirely unembarrassed with the calls of six Claviers upon his hands and feet, having at his immediate command the vast tonal forces (represented by ten thousand pipes) of this gigantic Organ; his hands simply engaged in manipulating the draw-stop knobs and combination buttons, and his feet controlling the flexible and expressive powers of the instrument. The Double Rolls do all the rest with a precision absolutely beyond the playing powers of the most skillful executant."

The organ is supplied with wind from five bellows; each bellows being 12 feet long and 6 feet wide. The bellows are furnished with wind from three square feeders set in motion by a shaft furnished with eccentrics, the feeders being operated by two 10 H. P. electric motors.

The Echo Organ feeders are operated by a one and one-half H. P. electric motor. The bellows is 12 feet long and 4 feet and three inches wide, it is supplied with wind by three square feeders which are operated by a three point shaft. The above blowing action is lubricated automatically. Every division of the organ has a regulating reservoir; these regulators supply the different organs with wind at a pressure of 4½, 7, 10 and 20 inches. The wind-chests have to furnish 10059 pipes with wind: they are 12 feet long and as broad as is required to give ample room for 140 stops. The material used in constructing the different wind conveyances is 20,000 feet of lumber for the wind-chests, 8,000 feet for the bellows and the feeders, and 2,000 feet for the wind trunks. The Swell boxes are very large, thus making every pipe easy of access for the tuner. There are five swell boxes, and they contain 7,500 feet of sugar pine. The organ has 1,300 magnets for key and draw stop actions. The magnets and couplers contain 130 miles of wire. The swell folds are operated by five electric engines. The organ contains 7,000 open circuits. The single contact system is used. The contacts of the coupler action clean themselves. Batteries of four cells each are used, with a capacity of two volts each. The ampere discharge is about 50 per eight hours. The batteries are charged with a motor generator of 220 volts direct current to a capacity of 10 volts, and 40 amperes. Charging the batteries in this manner does away with rheostat or lamps, thus preventing any loss of current. The motor generator always supplies amperes enough to allow using the organ continuously without any hitch.

The switch board is furnished with a volt and ammeter to show the strength of batteries. The ammeter shows the amount of electricity being used. The polarity indicator shows whether the electricity is being pumped into the batteries or out of them. A pilot lamp indicates the strength of batteries. The cut off switch throws off the current when the organ is not in use.

The organ is constructed under the W. B. Fleming patent. The automatic combination knobs number 1616; these are used for setting combinations in any portion of the organ. There are 36 couplers, 46 piston combinations, five tremulants, seven balanced swell pedals—two being for the grand crescendo.

The metal pipes contain 16,000 pounds of zinc and 9,000 pounds of soft metal. The wood pipes are made of California Sugar Pine and contain 35,000 feet of lumber. The frame is constructed of 3x12 inch Oregon Pine and contains 7,000 feet. It required twelve large furniture cars to move the organ from Los Angeles to St. Louis.

Prior to the construction of the organ by the Los Angeles company the Town Hall organ in Sydney, New South Wales, was the largest organ in the world; and this contains 126 speaking stops. This instrument was built in England in 1889. The largest organs in Boston, Massachusetts, are those in the church of the Immaculate Conception and Symphony Hall, each containing 56 stops, and the Shawmut Congregational Church containing 59 stops.

Specification of the Grand Concert Organ

"PEDAL ORGAN.
CCC to C—32 Notes.
M—Metal. W—Wood. R—Ranks

		Feet
1	Gravissima (result two lower octaves) .... W	64
2	Double Open Diapason (from Gt. No. 1) .... M	32
3	Double Open Diapason ...... W	32
4	Contra-Bourdon .... W	32
5	Open Diapason .... W	16
6	Open Diapason .... M	16
7	Violone .... M	16
8	Gamba .... M	16
9	Dulciana (express., from Ch. No. 1) .... M	16
10	Bourdon .... W	16
11	Lieblichgedeckt (express., from Sw. No. 12) .... W	16
12	Contrafluto .... W	16
13	Quintaten .... W	16

14	Quint	W	10 2-3
15	Octave	M	8
16	Dolce	M	8
17	Violoncello	M	9
18	Bass Flute	W	8
19	Weitgedeckt	W	8
20	Super-Octave	M	4
21	Offenflote	W	4
22	Compensating Mixture	M	VI R.
23	Contra-Bombarde	W	32
24	Bombarde	M	16
25	Contra-Posaune	M	16
26	Contrafagotto (expressive, from Sw. No. 26)	W	16
27	Euphonium (free reed)	M	16
28	Tromba	M	8
29	Fagotto	M	8
30	Clarion	M	4

FIRST OR GREAT ORGAN
CC to c4—61 Notes.
FIRST SUBDIVISION—UNEXPRESSIVE.

M—Metal.   W—Wood.   R—Ranks.

			Feet
1	Sub-Principal	M	32
2	Double Open Diapason	M	16
3	Contra-Gamba	M	16
4	Sub-Quint	W	10 2-3
5	Grand Principal	M	8
6	Open Diapason, Major	M	8
7	Open Diapason, Minor	M	8
8	Open Diapason	W	8

9	Grand Flute	W	8
10	Doppelflote	W	8
11	Gamba (pure tin)	M	8
12	Octave, Major	M	4
13	Gambette	M	4

SECOND SUBDIVISION—EXPRESSIVE.

Inclosed in Swell Box No. 1

14	Grobgedeckt	W	8
15	Harmonic Flute	M	8
16	Quint	M	5 1-3
17	Octave, Minor	M	4
18	Harmonic Flute	M	4
19	Tierce	M	3 1-5
20	Octave Quint	M	2 2-3
21	Super Octave	M	2
22	Grand Cornet IV. Ranks	Seventeenth ... M	1 3-5
		Nineteenth .... M	1 1-3
		Septieme ...... M	1 1-7
		Twenty-second . M	1
23	Grand Mixture	M	VII R
24	Double Trumpet	M	16
25	Harmonic Trumpet	M	8
26	Harmonic Clarion	M	4

This Expressive Subdivision can be brought on or thrown off Great Organ clavier by thumb pistons, and it is also commanded by the Double Touch of the clavier, at the will of the performer.

SECOND or CHOIR ORGAN—EXPRESSIVE.

CC to c4—61 Notes.

Inclosed in Swell Box No. 1.

M—Metal. W—Wood. R—Ranks.

			Feet
1	Double Dulciana	M	16
2	Open Diapason	M	8
3	Geigenprincipal	M	8
4	Salicional (pure tin)	M	8
5	Keraulophone	M	8
6	Dulciana	M	8
7	Vox Angelica	M	8
8	Vox Celestis	M	8
9	Quintadena	M	8
10	Stopped Diapason	W	8
11	Concert Flute	W	8
12	Flauto d'Amore	W & M	4
13	Salicet (pure tin)	M	4
14	Piccolo	M	2
15	Dulciana Cornet	M	VI R.
16	Contra-Saxaphone	M	16
17	Saxaphone	W	8
18	Corno Inglese	M	8
19	Musette	M	4
20	Carillon (Tublar bells)	M	

This Division of the Organ is commanded by the direct action of its own clavier, and is also commanded by the clavier of the Great Organ through the Double Touch of that clavier.

THIRD OR SWELL ORGAN.
CC to c4—61 Notes.
FIRST SUBDIVISION — EXPRESSIVE
Inclosed in Swell Box No. 2.
M—Metal. W—Wood. R—Ranks.

			Feet	
1	Lieblichgedeckt	W	16	
2	Horn Diapason	M	8	
3	Violin Diapason	M	8	
4	Grossflote	W	8	
5	Clarabella	W	8	
6	Doppelrohrgedeckt	W	8	
7	Melodia	W	8	
8	Flute Harmonique	M	8	
9	Dolce	M	8	
10	Gedecktquint	M	5	1-3
11	Octave	M	4	
12	Flute Harmonique	M	4	
13	Piccolo Harmonique	M	2	
14	Full Mixture (with covered ranks)	M	VI R.	
15	Contrafagotto	W	16	
16	Contra-Oboe	M	16	
17	Fagotto	W & M	8	
18	Orchestral Oboe	M	8	
19	Clarinet	M	8	
20	Corno di Bassetto	M	8	
21	Horn	M	8	
22	Vox Humana (two ranks)	W & M	8	
23	Octave Oboe	M	4	

This First Subdivision can be brought on or thrown off the Swell Organ clavier by thumb pistons.

SECOND SUBDIVISION—EXPRESSIVE.

Inclosed in Swell Box No. 3.

M—Metal. W—Wood. R—Ranks.

			Feet
24	Contra-Basso	W	16
25	Violoncello	pure tin	8
26	Viola	"	8
27	Violino	"	8
28	Violino (tuned slightly sharp)	"	8
29	Tiercena	"	8
30	Quint Viol	"	5 1-3
31	Octave Viol	"	4
32	Violette	"	4
33	Viol Cornet IV. Ranks { Viol, muted	"	2 2-3
	Viol,	"	2
	Viol,	"	1 3-5
	Viol,	"	1
34	Corroborating Mix. (string tone)	"	V R,

This Second, String-toned Subdivision can be brought on or thrown off the Swell Organ clavier by thumb pistons; and it is also commanded by the Double Touch of the clavier.

FOURTH OR SOLO ORGAN—EXPRESSIVE.
CC to c4—61 Notes.
Inclosed in Swell Box No. 4.
M—Metal. W—Wood. R—Ranks.

			Feet
1	Double Open Diapason	M	16
2	Flute a Pavillon	M	8
3	Stentorphone	M	8
4	Grossgambe (pure tin)	M	8
5	Grossflote	W	8
6	Doppeloffenflote	W	8
7	Orchestral Flute	W	8
8	Harmonic Flute	M	4
9	Octave	M	4
10	Grand Cornet	M IV, V & VI	R.
11	Bass Trombone	M	16
12	Bass Tuba	M	16
13	Trombone	M	8
14	Ophicleide	M	8
15	Orchestral Trumpet	M	8
16	Orchestral Clarinet (2 ranks)	W & M	8
17	Harmonic Clarion	M	4
18	Drums		

FIFTH OR ECHO ORGAN—EXPRESSIVE.
CC to c4—61 Notes.
Inclosed in Swell Box No. 5.
M—Metal. W—Wood. R—Ranks.

			Feet
1	Stillgedeckt	W	16
2	Echo Diapason	M	8

3 Nachthorn ....M 8
4 Spitzflote ....M 8
5 Viola d'Amore ....M 8
6 Harmonica ....W 8
7 Unda Maris ....M 8
8 Flauto d'Amore ....W 4
9 Gemshorn ....M 4
10 Echo Cornet ....M V R.
11 Echo Trumpet ....M 8
12 Vox Humana (two ranks) W & M 8

This Organ is to be located at a considerable distance from the main portion of the instrument.

MECHANICAL APPLIANCES
PEDAL COUPLERS.

1 Great Organ, 1st subdivision, to Pedal Organ
2 Great Organ, 2nd subdivision, to Pedal Organ
3 Choir Organ to Pedal Organ
4 Swell Organ, 1st subdivision, to Pedal Organ
5 Swell Organ, 2nd subdivision, to Pedal Organ
6 Solo Organ to Pedal Organ
7 Echo Organ to Pedal Organ
8 Pedal, Octave Coupler on itself

MANUAL COUPLERS
UNISON COUPLERS.

1 Choir Organ to Great Organ
2 Swell Organ, 1st subdivision, to Great Organ

3 Swell Organ, 2nd subdivision, to Great Organ
4 Solo Organ to Great Organ
5 Echo Organ to Great Organ
6 Swell Organ, 1st subdivision, to Choir Organ
7 Swell Organ, 2nd subdivision, to Choir Organ
8 Solo Organ to Choir Organ
9 Echo Organ to Choir Organ
10 Solo Organ to Swell Organ
11 Echo Organ to Swell Organ

SUB-OCTAVE COUPLERS.

1 Swell Organ, 2nd subdivision, to Great Organ
2 Choir Organ to Great Organ
3 Solo Organ to Great Organ
4 Great Organ, Sub-Octave Coupler on itself
5 Swell Organ, Sub-Octave Coupler
6 Choir Organ, Sub-Octave Coupler on itself

OCTAVE COUPLERS.

1 Choir Organ to Great Organ
2 Swell Organ, 1st subdivision, to Great Organ
3 Swell Organ, 2nd subdivision, to Great Organ
4 Solo Organ to Great Organ
5 Echo Organ to Great Organ
6 Great Organ, Octave Coupler on itself
7 Choir Organ, Octave Coupler on itself

8 Swell Organ, Octave Coupler on itself
9 Solo Organ, Octave Coupler on itself
10 Echo Organ, Octave Coupler on itself

TREMOLANTS.

1 Tremolant to Choir Organ
2 Tremolant to 1st subdivision of Swell Organ
3 Tremolant to 2nd subdivision of Swell Organ
4 Tremolant to Solo Organ
5 Tremolant to Echo Organ

ADJUSTABLE COMBINATION ACTION.

Commanded by thumb pistons located between the manual claviers.

1 2 3 4 0	Operating on First Subdivision of Great and Pedal
1 2 3 4 0	Operating on Second Subdivision of Great and Pedal
1 2 3 4 5 0	Operating on First Subdivision of Swell and Pedal
1 2 3 4 5 0	Operating on Second Subdivision of Swell and Pedal
1 2 3 4 5 6 0	Operating on Choir and Pedal
1 2 3 4 5 0	Operating on Solo and Pedal
1 2 3 4 0	Operating on Echo and Pedal

1 2 3 4 5 6   Operating on any combinations of stops or solo stops as may be desired

General Release
Pedal Release

PEDAL MOVEMENTS.

1. Balanced Expression-pedal to Swell-box No. 1
2. Balanced Expression-pedal to Swell-box No. 2
3. Balanced Expression-pedal to Swell-box No. 3
4. Balanced Expression-pedal to Swell-box No. 4
5. Balanced Expression-pedal to Swell-box No. 5
6. Locking-pedal connecting all Expression-pedals to Expression-pedal No. 1
7. Balanced Crescendo-pedal, operating on each Manual Division separately
8. Balanced Crescendo-pedal, operating on the Full Organ and all Couplers
9. Locking-pedal, reducing the Pedal Organ from forte to piano
10. Reversible Pedal, operating Great Organ to Pedal Organ

SUMMARY.

PEDAL ORGAN	...30 Stops	...1152 Pipes
GREAT	"	...26	"	...2135 "
CHOIR	"	...20	"	...1501 "
SWELL	"	...34	"	...2867 "
SOLO	"	...18	"	...1367 "
ECHO	"	...12	"	...1037 "

Total Speaking Stops, 140   Pipes, 10,059
Mechanical appliances, 99, as above set forth"

Compensating Pipe Organ

In this organ the tone is produced through a combination of pipes and reeds. The pipes used are the ordinary pipes of the pipe organ, and the reeds are the free reeds such as are used in the parlor organ. The difficulty of combining reeds and pipes in the same instrument is that the pipes change in pitch as the temperature varies; this has been overcome in the Compensating Pipe Organ by a mechanical device that is easy to operate. With this contrivance the organ can be kept in tune as the temperature varies.

The Piano-Player

The Piano-Player is a pneumatic instrument; its mechanism consists of diaphragms, primary and secondory valves, and pneumatics used to actuate the keys of the piano.

Early Types of Players

Among the early types of players was the Pianista invented by a Frenchman named Fourneaux, and patented in 1863. The motive power or air was supplied by a bellows operated by turning a crank or pumping with the feet. In 1878 an automatic piano-player was patented by Merritt Gally. In this instrument there were means for governing the power of the stroke on the piano keys. This invention was due to American ingenuity. Since this time there have been many improvements. All pneumatic piano-players use air on the exhaust principal. (See Reed Organ, 124.)

The Pneumatic Motor

The motor is used to roll and re-roll the perforated music sheet; there are two kinds in general use, the wind and the spring motor. The wind motor consists of three or five small bellows which revolve a shaft that in turn operates the music roll. These small bellows are set in motion by the air being drawn through them into the exhaust; the latter is operated by means of foot pedals. In this style of player the bellows must not only exhaust the air from the key pneumatics but also from the motors which require about forty per cent of the air exhausted. This additional force must be furnished by the performer. For this reason the player operated in this manner requires extra effort.

The Spring Motor

The spring motor consists of a spring and clock works controlled by a governor to give a uniform speed, which can be changed instantly by moving a lever from right to left. In this style of player fast and slow pumping does not change the tempo.

Parts of the Piano-Player
(See Figure 14, page 170.)

1. Pedal; its use is to operate the exhaust. 2. Pedal strap; its use is to connect

Fig. 14

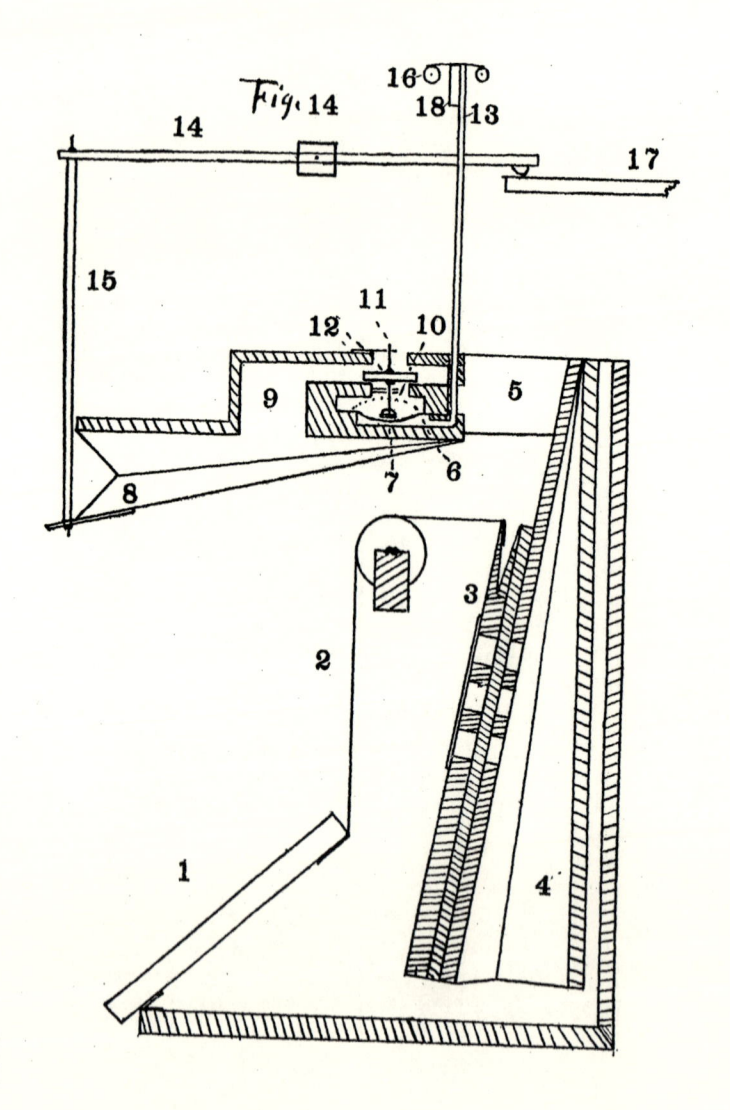

pedal and exhaust. In the later players this strap is not used, the connection being made with a metal rod fastened directly to the exhaust. In this case the exhaust is fastened in a horizontal position instead of being perpendicular. 3. Exhauster; its use is to pump the air out of the bellows 4. 4. Bellows; when the air is pumped out of the bellows the back board of the bellows moves toward the exhaust. This board has attached to it two springs for the purpose of forcing the board back to its normal position; and this backward motion of the board caused by the force of the springs creates a vacuum. The vacuum thus created is used to collapse the pneumatic 8. 5. Wind or exhaust trunk; this is used to connect bellows 4 and exhaust chest 10. 6. Diaphragm chamber; the air in this chamber is partly exhausted, and it is separated from the exhaust chest 10 by a diaphragm or pouch; the only communication between chamber 6 and the exhaust chest 10 is through a very small bleed hole not shown in the cut. The purpose of this bleed hole is to partially exhaust the air from the chamber 6 as above stated. 7. Disk; this disk is screwed to the lower end of the spindle, and its use is to regulate the motion of the puppet-valve 12. 8. Pneumatic; the use of the pneumatic is to furnish the motive power which operates the key. 9. Exhaust and inflate channel; through this channel the air passes, in exhausting and inflating the pneumatic 8. 10. Exhaust chest; when the player is in use the space in this chest forms a complete vacuum. 11. Spindle; the lower end of the spindle is screwed into disk 7, while the upper end passes through a guide which serves as a support to the spindle; the use of this spindle is to operate the puppet-valve. 12. 12. Puppet-valve; its use is to cover and uncover the opening of the exhaust chest 10 and inflate and exhaust channel 9, 13. Vent duct or tube; this is an air passage from the tracker range 18 to the diaphragm chamber 6. 14. Key finger or lever. 15. Sticker. 16. Music sheet roll; on which the sheet is rolled as it passes over the tracker-board 18. 17. Piano-key. 18. Tracker-board; the face of this board is provided with ducts, one for each pneumatic.

How the Player is Operated

When the upper end of the vent duct or tube 13 is uncovered by a perforation in the music sheet a puff of air passes down the tube to the diaphragm chamber 6; the diaphragm is a flexible piece of leather shown in the cut by a full line directly under the dotted lines in chest 10. The diaphragm answers a double purpose, in addition to operating the puppet-valve it serves as a cover to chamber 6. The air in this chamber forms a partial vacuum and offers less resistance than that of chest 10.

When a perforation in the music sheet passes over an opening in the tracker-board 18, thereby admitting air into the duct 13, and thus destroying the partial vacuum in chamber 6, the diaphragm is raised or drawn up by the complete exhaust or vacuum in chest 10, to the position indicated by the dotted lines; thus causing the disk 7, to lift the spindle 11, thereby lifting the puppet-valve 12. When the puppet-valve reaches the top of the exhaust channel 9, it closes the opening and at the same instant opens the one on the bottom, thus establishing communication between the exhaust chest 10 and the pneumatic 8. This immediately exhausts pneumatic 8 thereby causing it to collapse. The pneumatic in collapsing lifts the movable board or flap. With this board is connected the lower end of the sticker 15, and the upper end of the sticker is fastened to the front end of the key lever 14. This upward motion of the sticker moves the front end of the key lever up, thereby causing the back end to go down, and this communicates its motion to the key 17, thus causing it to sound.

Pneumatic Piano-Player Action
(See Figure 15, page 174)

1. Pedal. 2. Exhaust spring. 3. Exhaust. 4. Exhaust-valve. This valve allows the air to escape after it has been pumped out of the bellows. There is another valve placed on the middle-board to prevent the air from

Fig. 15

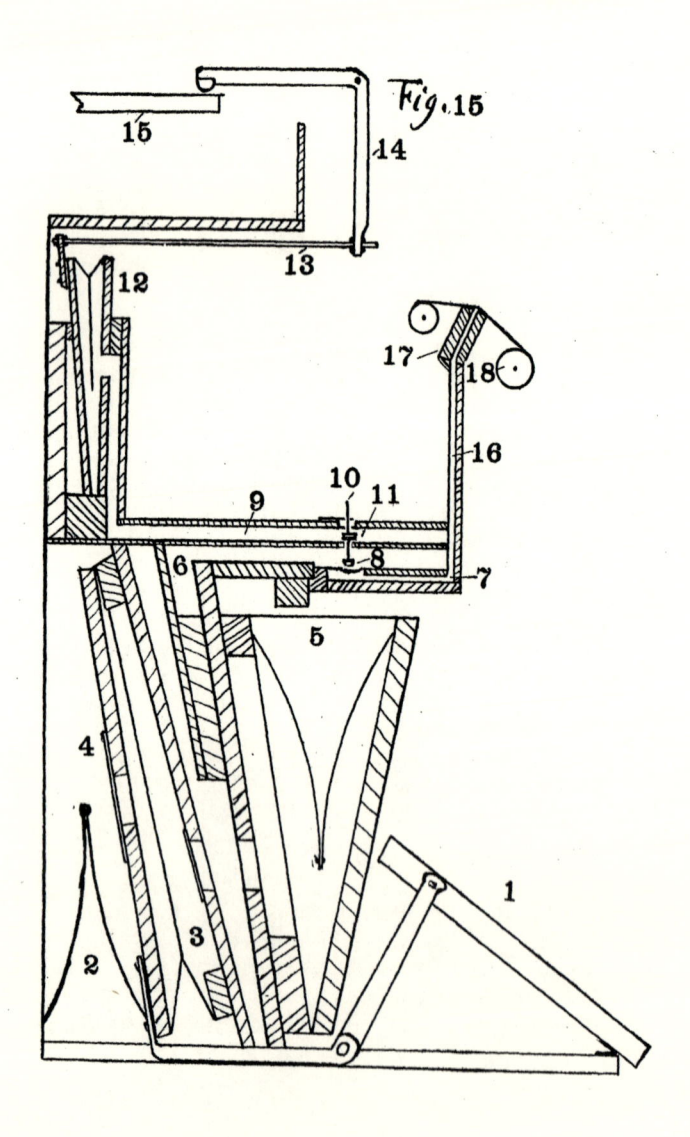

rushing back into the bellows after it has been pumped out; this valve is directly above No. 3 in the exhaust. 5. Bellows. 6. Exhaust chest. When the player is in use the air has been pumped out of this chest, thus forming a vacuum; the function of this vacuum is to operate the puppet-valve and pneumatic. 7. Diaphragm chamber. There is a small vent hole from this chamber to exhaust chest 6, for the purpose of partially exhausting the air. The complete vacuum of chest 6 being more powerful than the partial vacuum of chamber 7, it raises the diaphragm. This is accomplished in the following way; when a perforation in the music sheet passes over a duct in the tracker-board the air rushes down the exhaust tube 16 and destroys the vacuum in chamber 7, and owing to the fact of the vacuum in chest 6 being the stronger of the two it draws up the diaphragm which is twice the size of the valve which nearly rests on the diaphragm; and the diaphragm being the larger of the two can raise the puppet-valve 11, which in turn shuts off the external air thus establishing communication between exhaust chest 6 and the exhuast and inflate channel 9; the vacuum in chest 6 now exhausts the air from pneumatic 12 and thus causes it to collapse. This motion of the pneumatic carries with it the sticker 13 which in turn is connected to the square or key finger, and this backward motion of the lower end of the key finger moves the upper end down under which rests the piano key. 8. Disk; which regulates the lower end of spindle 10. 9. Exhaust and inflate channel; through which air passes to exhaust and inflate the pneumatic 12. 10. Spindle; to which is fastened the puppet valve 11. 11. Puppet-valve; its use is to open and close valve hole of chest 6 and channel 9. 12. Striking pneumatic; its use is to operate the key finger. 13. Sticker; its use is to connect pneumatic and key finger. 14. Square or key finger; its use is to operate the key. 15. Piano key. 16. Vent duct or tube; through which a puff of air passes when duct of 17 is uncovered by the music sheet; this puff of external air passing through chamber 7, to the diaphragm with the aid of the vacuum in chest 6, raises the diaphragm, as air rushing in or out of a pneumatic aided by a vacuum acts like an explosion. 17. Tracker-board. 18. Music sheet roll.

Simplex Player
(See Figure 16, page 177.)

1. Showing position of gaues; its use is to prevent dust or fibre from the music sheet, that might be drawn in through the tracker-board 5, from making its way up to the bleed hole 2, and thereby closing it. 2. Bleed hole; its use is to draw the air out of the channel leading from the tracker-board 5, to diaphragm 3; this channel from tracker-board to diaphragm must have a vent to permit the diaphragm's return after

Fig. 16

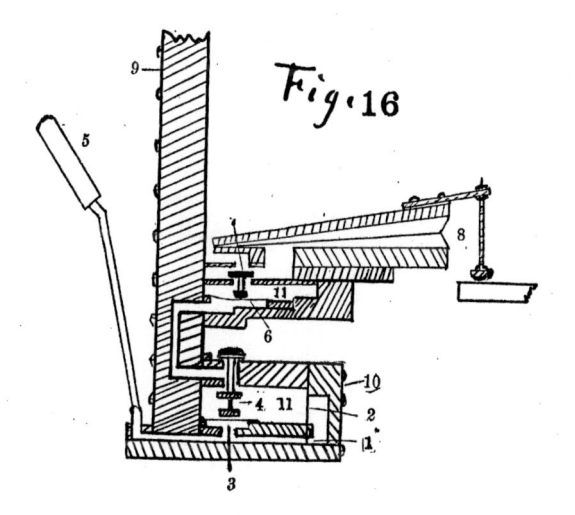

the music sheet has closed the opening in the tracker-board. 3. Primary Diaphragm; its use is to raise primary valve 4. 4. Primary valve; its use is to exhaust and fill the channel with air between primary 4 and secondary diaphragm 6. 5. Tracker-board; over which the perforated music sheet passes. 6. Secondary Diaphragm; its use is to lift secondary valve 7. 7. Secondary valve; its use is to close the opening on top of valve thereby preventing external air from making its way into pneumatic 8, and also at the same time uncovering the opening at the under side of the valve, thus allowing the vacuum to draw the air out of the pneumatic 8 and thereby collapsing it. 8. Pneumatic; its use is to operate the piano key. 9 and 10. Channel boards. 11. Vacuum chamber.

Reasons Why the Pneumatic Will Not Act

When dust has been sucked in the duct ports and has lodged on the vent or bleed holes, thereby closing them, and thus destroying communication between the exhaust diaphragm and pouch chamber. Remedy: remove the channel board and clean the gaues. The groove leading to the vent or bleed hole is usually covered with a fine wire screen to prevent the dust from passing into the bleed hole and thereby closing it. The secondary valve will not act when the lower end of spindle 10, Figure 15, page 174, is screwed into disk too far, thus causing too much space between the disk and diaphragm, and thereby preventing the disk from lifting the puppet-valve far enough to close the opening on top of the valve. Remedy: unscrew the spindle far enough for it to work properly. When the leather of the pneumatic diaphragm or pouch is too thick or stiff, it will cause repetition to be poor, especially in piano passages. The pneumatic will not return when the pneumatic spring is too weak or broken, and also when the guide wires of pneumatic are bent.

Reasons Why the Pneumatic Acts When It Should not

When a hole is in the rubber tube, or there is any leakage leading to the primary or secondary valve, the channel board screws being loose will result in a leak, and cause the pneumatic to act. When the diaphragm or pouch of the primary or secondary valve contracts, thus raising the valve enough to operate the pneumatic. Remedy: regulate the disk by turning it up; if this cannot be done put in new pouch. To regulate the disk use two saw files, placing one on each side of the disk. By drawing on one and pushing on the other the disk can be raised or lowered as required. Do not allow the files to touch the diaphragm or pouch, as there is danger of puncturing it. When any foreign substance has lodged between the diaphragm and disk of the primary or secondary valve. (For directions, see the

Cleaning of the Player, see below.) When a groove is unsound: glue sheep-skin over crack. If the leather on the bellows squeaks, rub a little vaseline on the leather where it folds. For faults of bellows and exhaust, see Reed Organ, page 127. If the music roll will not wind or unwind the music sheet, the trouble is in the chain or motor; in the chain jumping from sprocket wheel, or becoming twisted, or the sprocket wheel becoming loose on the shaft, or friction too great on the motor shaft, or motor valves disarranged, or screws loose, that fasten motor to wind-chest. In some players the motor shaft is furnished with three eccentrics, in others five. If a spring motor is used it may need cleaning and oiling. The friction wheel of the spool that rewinds the music may be covered with a sticky substance. Remedy: clean the wheel and put on a little machine oil; this wheel is provided with a tension spring sufficient to hold the music sheet on the tracker board with force enough not to allow air to pass between the board and paper.

Player: How Cleaned

A player should be thoroughly cleaned every few years and re-regulated. The system of operation being exhaust, it draws or sucks dust and other obstructions into it; the obstruction lodging on the valves and in the air passages, and closing them and interfering with their action. This difficulty shows itself in slowness of repetition, and is remedied by taking off the channel boards, cleaning all primary and secondary valves, and blowing all dust out of the tubes and channels. The valves can be cleaned by use of No. 18 piano wire bent over at the end in the form of a hook; passing the bent portion of the wire between the valves and the chest will remove all obstruction.

The Pianola Player

The key levers are raised to the required height by turning screws placed in the sides of the case, with a wrench provided for that purpose. Turn the screws toward the piano at the treble end and away from the piano at the bass end, to raise the key levers. When they are properly adjusted there should be a space of one-sixteenth of an inch between the cushion on the end of the key lever and the ivory on the key.

The Pianola: How to Take It Apart

In most cases the trimmings of the case both front and back must be removed; also the top of the case. The screws that hold the top pass up from the under side on the front of the case directly below the cover of the music roll, and there are also two hooks placed on the inside of the case one at each end. To reach these hooks take out the portion of the case under the key levers, next take off the back panel, next take the pump irons off the exhausts, then take out the screws that hold the exhausts to the bellows, next take out screws that hold the bellows to the pneumatic chest, next take out the screws that hold pneumatic chest to the sides of the case: the pneumatic chest can now be taken out, by lifting it up through the top of the case.

How to Take off Channel Board

First remove the levers just below the tracker-board, then take screws out of the channel-board; this board is known by the great number of screws it contains. After the channel board has been removed, the primary and secondary valves can be reached if they need attention. Should there be any obstruction under the top of the primary valve the board that serves as a cover to the primaries must be taken off: this board also has attached to it the tracker-board, spool, and wind motor. The screws that hold this board are at each end and the side directly under the key fingers; also one large screw is at the upper edge of the finger rail; after this screw has been taken out the board with the tracker range and wind motor attached can be removed.

Parts of the Pianola

(See Figure 17, page 183.)

1. Diaphragm chambers. 2. Bleed hole.
3. Primary Diaphragm. 4. Primary disk.
5. Tracker-board. 6. Secondary Diaphragm.
8. Pneumatic. 11. Vacuum chests.

Fig. 17

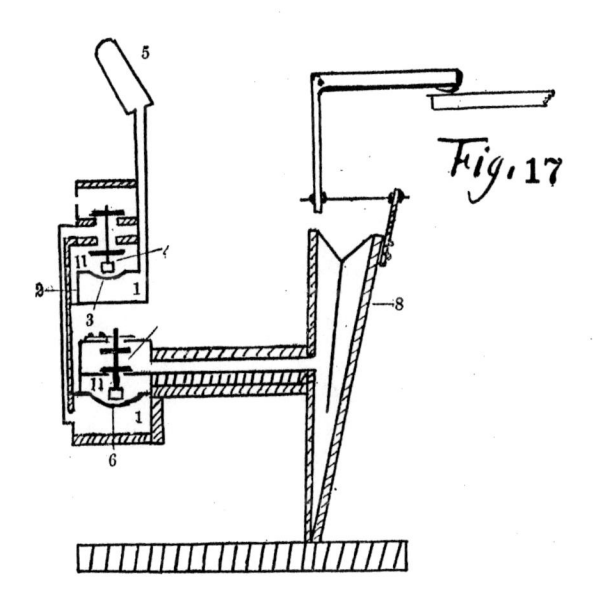

Tuning the Aeolian Piano

Before tuning remove the motor; this is done by taking out three screws that pass through brackets supporting the motor. Next disconnect the large rubber tube, that operates the motor, where it is joined to the metal elbow; also remove the motor chain. If the thumping rail is resting on the keys, it can be raised by throwing off the stop under the key-bed at the treble end of key-board.

Aeolian Interior Player

The pneumatic action in this player is exactly the same as for the Pianola. To take out the piano action remove the tracker-board and pneumatic motor; this is done by taking out the screws at the right of motor, where the large rubber tube connects with the end pneumatic of motor. It is easier to slip the tube from the elbow at end of the case. Next take out the screws at each end of rail that supports the tracker-board and the motor; also the screws of the braces in the piano plate. Next remove the shelf and fall-board. The tracker-board can now be laid down on the key-board of the piano providing that the tubes are made of rubber that lead from the tracker-board to the primary valves.

To Put in New Strings and Fix Squeaking Pedals

For such repairs it is necessary to take out the pumping action which is directly back of the bottom frame, and is held in position by screws placed at each end of the frame both at its top and the bottom. Next take out the screws that hold the large rubber tubes to the bellows, then disconnect all expressive levers; the pumping action is now free and can be removed. After this has been done there is room enough to pass the hand between the pneumatic chest and the strings to replace them if they are broken. If the pneumatic action needs attention, the channel board can be easily taken off as it is directly above the pumping action.

The Simplex Player

The key levers on the Simplex are raised by thumb screws placed on the under side of the case. To raise the levers turn the screws in. If the key levers have been raised as high as the screws will carry them and yet they are too low to pass over the keys, they can be regulated by turning the leather nuts farther in on the threaded wire of the key lever.

Pneumatic-chest: How to Take Out

Remove all trimmings, also the top of the case; the screws that hold the top are on the inside of the front of the case close to the wind trunks at each end of the pneumatic chest. Next displace the chains of the spool and re-roll sprockets, then take out the screws that pass into the tracker-board. Next take off the brace at lower end of tracker-board cheeks; also the screws that pass from the cheeks that go into the pneumatic chest. Next take out the music roll or spool; the screw that holds the spool is placed at the right, passing into the sprocket shaft. Next take out the tracker-board cover: this is done by pulling out the pin at each end of the cover where it passes through cheeks. The tracker-board can now be lowered and slipped out from cheeks; this leaves the tracker-board and tubes attached to the pneumatic chest, with which they are removed. Next take off the wind trunks at each end of the chest. Next take out the screws that pass through cleats into the upper portion of the chest both on the front and the back of the chest; this leaves the chest free, so that it can now be taken out by lifting it up through the top of the case. If the valves and the pneumatics need repairs, take off the channel board by removing the screws which are quite numerous. If the primaries are obstructed or need regulating in this instrument it is not necessary to take out the pneumatic chest to repair them, as they can be adjusted by taking out the screws that hold in the bung, directly under the key fingers; after this has been removed the primaries are easy of access. (See Player; How Cleaned, page 180.)

Spring Motor Noisy

When a spring motor is used, if the spring is noisy or squeaks, sprinkle powdered graphite in through the openings in the side of the spring case left for that purpose.

Motor Will Not Run

When the spring shaft binds where it passes through spring case. Remedy this by filing the shaft enough to prevent friction, then smooth the shaft at points of bearing with emery cloth. To lubricate, use a good grade of machine oil.

How to Take Out the Player Action

In most players the trimmings of the case, both front and back, must be removed as also must the top of the case. The screws that hold the top of the case are usually on the inside and can be taken out after the trimmings have been removed. In some cases it is not necessary to remove the top of the case in order to take out the action. After the trimmings, top and connecting rods, metronome, roll and re-roll, piano and forte, and also the sustaining pedal, have been set aside, the action of the player can be removed by taking out screws that hold it to the case. In some players the action lifts up through the top of the case, in others it comes out through the front of the case. After the action has been taken out, the channel board can be removed; this board is known by the number of screws that fasten it to the chest. After this has been done, if the diaphragms, valves and pneumatics need repairing they are easy of access.

Player: How Affected by Moisture and Heat

In the winter when the air is heated artificially the wood work that the pouch or diaphragm is fastened to shrinks, and this causes the diaphragm to tighten, thereby raising it and in some instances enough to come in contact with the disk or button on the lower end of the primary valve which will open the valve a trifle on top and cause it to leak. If this leak is sufficient, it will exhaust the secondary valve which in turn will exhaust the pneumatic and cause it to make the key speak. If the leak thus caused is not enough to operate the pneumatic it will result in poor accent, because of the fact that the air drawing through the valves is sufficient to offset the extra force required for accenting.

In the summer months when the wood is affected by moisture the diaphragm will hang too low and cannot reach the disk or button on the primary valve, and this will destroy the repetition of the action; it will also require pumping very fast to operate the player. The valves are regulated by the use of saw files as already stated on page 94. For this reason a player may work all right to-day and all wrong to-morrow.

The Angelus Player
(See Figure 18, page 189.)

In this instrument the device for raising and lowering the finger rail M is as follows: The ends of the rail that support the

Fig 18

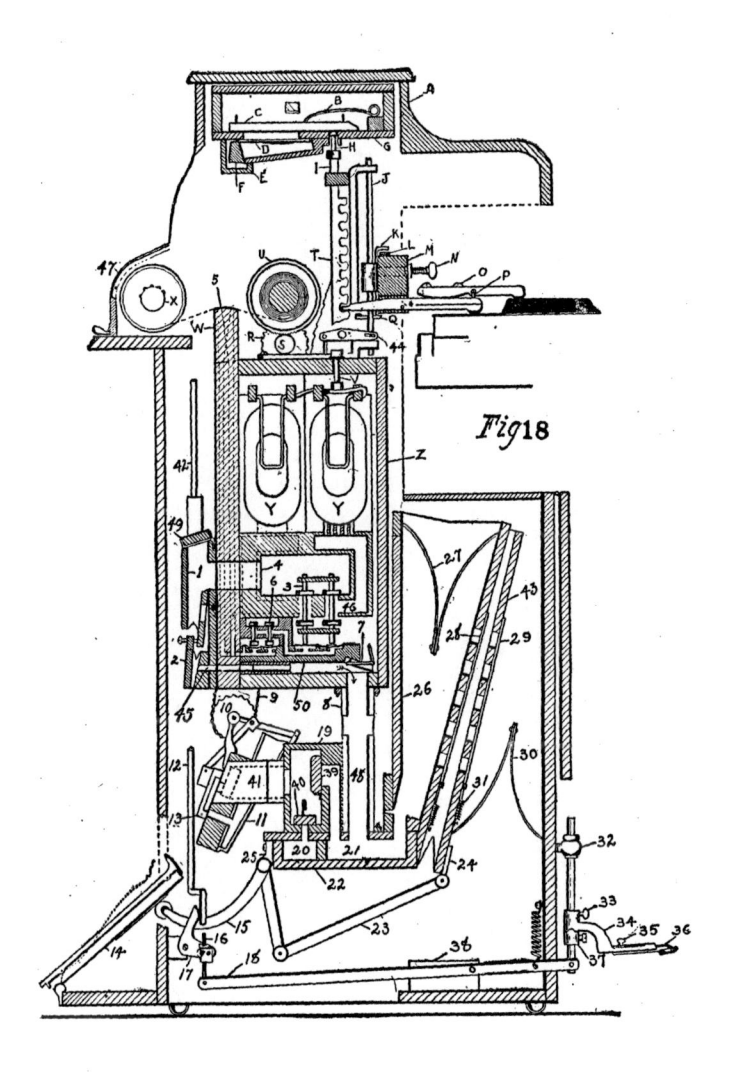

fingers can be moved up and down on guide rods J placed at each end of the rail. The finger lever at the back end is shaped like the damper lever of the Old English square piano, and the lifter or standard T from the pneumatic is shaped like the tail of the key; these fit into each other when in position. The finger lever is covered with felt to prevent rattling. The lifter from the pneumatic is an upright piece of wood furnished with nine notches, for the interchangeable engagement of the ends of the finger levers. In a player of this style the finger levers can be raised or lowered without changing the position of the pneumatic action, motor, bellows or the case of the instrument, to any point desired to suit the height of any key board. To raise and lower key fingers loosen lock nuts N on thumb screws fastened in finger rail, then unscrew thumb screws enough to free the finger rail; after which the rail can be raised or lowered as desired. To regulate the fingers accurately they are furnished with screws O, P. On the extreme front end these screws should be so adjusted that the cushion on the finger will rest the thickness of a postal card above the ivory on the key of the piano. The pneumatics are glued in grooves and can be taken out after the strips that pass over their tops have been removed; by tilting the pneumatics from side to side the glue will give way, thus freeing the pneumatic which can now be taken out for repairs. The tubes leading from the tracker-board to the primary chamber are liable to be choked, and this will result in slowness of action. They can be cleaned when they are filled with fibre from the music sheet by using a two ounce hard rubber syringe. Fasten a short piece of rubber tubing to the syringe large enough in diameter to cover two holes in the tracker-board. Place the rubber over the holes and operate the piston: the force and suction of the syringe will remove all obstruction.

How the Key Levers or Fingers are Fastened

To take out one or more fingers or key levers, remove the rail directly over the fingers. This rail is held in place with a screw at each end, also one in the centre of the rail. The centre screw can be taken out with a double headed or ratchet screw-driver. Next disconnect the stop lever at the treble end of the rail. After this rail has been removed, the screws that hold the fingers are easy of access, and can be taken out with a small short screw-driver, (usually sent with the player for that purpose.) The screw that holds the finger to the rail cuts down in the finger and cannot be seen. After the screw has been taken out the finger is free for needed repairs. If a finger is warped and strikes two keys, it can be set back in place by taking out the warped finger, and bending the pin that guides the back end of the finger. Doing this will move the front end of the finger into its proper position.

Tuning the Piano to the Angelus

If the Orchestral attachment of the Angelus is used with the piano, the piano must be tuned to the Angelus. To ascertain the pitch of the reeds, cover the tracker-board with a piece of paper, or draw the Re-Roll stop. If the tracker-board of 58 ducts is used, fasten down the 25th finger, one line C¹, counting both the short and the long fingers from the bass up. If the tracker-board of 65 ducts is used, lower the 28 finger which is also one line C¹. Tune to the Melodia or Orchestral stop.

Explanation of Figure 18
(See Figure 18, page 189.)

A   Case
B   Reed valve spring (Angelus Orchestral)
C   Reed valve   "
D   Reed   "
E   Swell box   "
F   Mute   "
G   Reed chamber   "
H   Reed pitman   "
I   Reed pitman lifter   "
J   Iron brackets for supporting fingers
K   Evener wire
L   Evener rail
M   Finger rail
N   Thumb nut
O   Regulating screws (long fingers)
P   "   "   (short fingers)
Q   Finger rest

R Sprocket on top shaft
S Gear on top shaft
T Plungers
U Large gear on take-up roll
V Power pneumatic buttons
W Tracker
X Sprocket on star wheel clutch
Y Power pneumatics
Z Pneumatic action chest

Explanation of Motor Governor
(See Figure 19, page 194.)

2 Phrasing lever connection
3 Spring connection
4 Spring
5 Regulating screw
6 Spring holder
7 Pneumatic
20-21-22 see Fig. 18. page 189.

---

1 Choker pneumatic (large)
2 Choker   "   (small)
3 Secondary valves
4 Port to outside air
5 Tracker cap or mouthpiece (showing air passages)
6 Primary valves
7 Pneumatic action chest valve
8 Air conductor from bellows to chest
9 Sprocket chain (motor to top shaft)
10 Motor sprocket wheel
11 Motor feeders (pneumatic)
12 Sustaining pedal wire
13 Sliding motor valves

Fig. 19

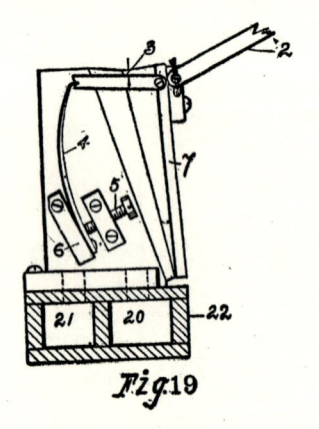

14 Foot pedal
15 Foot pedal iron
16 Adjustable connection to sustaining pedal
17 Pedal elbow
18 Pedal lever
19 Gate box
20 Air port from motor. Air is admitted to this port through the motor governor (not shown, see Fig. 19).
21 Air port to bellows
22 Lower conductor
23 Connection (feeder to pedal iron)
24 Feeder irons
25 Pedal iron support
26 Bellows
27 Bellows spring
28 Bellows valve
29 Feeder valve
30 Feeder spring
31 Feeder valve spring
32-33-34-35-36-37-38 parts forming set sustaining piano pedal set
39 By pass valve
40 Metronome valve
41 Port from motor to gate box
42 Choker cover connection
43 Feeders
44 Lifter (Angelus Orchestral only)
45 Port to small choker pneumatic
46 Port to power pneumatics
47 Transparent cover over music
48 Port to pneumatic chest

49 Choker cover
50 Well board containing first and secondary pneumatics and vents

The Angelus: How to Take it Apart

The reed chest G is under the top of the case.

How to Take Out the Reeds

To take out the reeds remove the upper back panel, then lower the swell and stop mutes, F: the reeds can now be drawn by use of the reed hook. For faults of reeds see Reed Organ, page 130. The top of the case can be removed by taking out two screws that pass up at each end of the case almost over the rail that holds the finger rail: this frees the top which can now be removed. If the reed valves C need repairing, take off the top of the reed wind chest. For repairs on the exhaust and bellows remove the shelf and lower back panel. To take out the pneumatic chest Z remove the front panel, and also the board directly above the panel: then take off the truss at each end of the case. These are held in position by screws entering on the side. Next remove the chokers 1-2, and their operating levers 42. A choker is a small wooden case fastened to the front board of the pneumatic chest, and when used serves the purpose of reducing the flow of external air to the key pneumatic, thereby making it strike a softer blow. Next remove all expressive levers from the front board. Then take out the screws in front board which will free the board. After this board has been removed the pneumatic chest Z can be taken out by carefully drawing it forward, also tipping it slightly, just as is done in removing a drawer of a table. The various valves and pneumatics can now be adjusted or repaired if they need attention.

Music Sheet Does Not Track Properly

The Angelus is furnished with an appliance to adjust the music sheet when it does not track. This is done by turning a thumb screw placed in one of the cheeks of the tracker-board: turning this screw in or out moves the music to the right or left.

Angelus Interior Player Mechanism: How to Take It Out

The top frame of the piano case is removed the same as in the ordinary piano. To tune and mute the piano, drop back the motor; this is done by displacing motor chain and unscrewing the thumb nut at upper left end of the motor, thus allowing the motor to swing back enough to get at the wires. If more room is desired the motor can be removed by taking out the screw at each end that it swings on; it can now be placed on top of the piano case.

How to Remove Piano Action

Take out screws that pass into each end of the tracker-board. These screws pass through the sides of the motor, and spool case, then disconnect the upright rod that works in reel of the sprocket shaft nearly at the left end of shaft. Next take out the shelf screws by lifting the shelf slightly and moving it a little to the right: the sprocket shaft will then slip out of piano case. The shelf can then be raised and removed with the entire motor action attached. The piano action can now be taken out, but this must be done cautiously as the dampers are apt to strike the action bolts, and the jack-rockers are liable to interfere with the tracker-board tubes which are attached to the key bed and need not be removed.

How to Take Out Pneumatic Action

Remove all piano keys between the tracker-board tubes, then take out the screws that pass down through tube rail on key bed into the pneumatic chest. There are two rows of screws one on each side of the tubes. This will free the pneumatic chest from the tracker range. Next take off the spring on key bed that holds in the bottom frame; also take out the bottom frame. Next disconnect the rods to the choker muffler: these will be found at the lower right hand corner of the pneumatic chest. Notice which rod goes back as both rods are of same length and can be easily mixed. Next take off the muffler; this is done by turning the small wire hooks so that they stand opposite openings in the muffler; the muffler can now be removed.

Next take out the small piece of bottom frame to the right of the damper or sustaining pedal: this will allow getting at the screw on the lower end of the pneumatic chest directly above the piece just removed. Take out these screws; then with a short screw-driver reach in at the end of pneumatic chest where the muffler was and take out the screws that hold the chest and wind trunk together: these screws pass down into the wind trunk of the bellows. Next take out the screws at the lower left corner of the pneumatic chest; these screws pass through the chest into the wind trunk of the motor and will be found directly over the small piece of bottom frame at the left end of the case. Now by turning a button at the upper right and left hand corners of the pneumatic chest it can be taken out: this is done by slightly lifting and pulling out. If every thing is free it will come out easily, and after it has been removed the piano is free for stringing and other repairs that it may need.

Faults of Player

If the motor chain is too loose tighten it by turning out the nut of the bolt entering the pin block.

Primary and Secondary Valves

If these valves need attention, before disturbing them make a perpendicular pencil mark on each valve and frame just below it: this will often save a great deal of trouble as it frequently happens that when the position of the valves has been changed they will not seat perfectly, thus causing a leak. The pencil mark will show when valves are in the right position.

Lubricating Parts

Do not use any lubricant on valves or valve seats. When bearings need lubricating use a good machine oil. Do not apply oil until the bearings have been thoroughly cleaned; benzine and a piece of cloth are best suited for this purpose.

Pneumatic Does Not Act

If a pneumatic does not act, first see that all screws in the channel board and wind trunks and also the tracker range are tight. Second, see that the tube or duct from tracker-board to primary diaphragm is clear. Third see that the vent or bleed hole is not choked. Fourth see that the primary valve works freely. Fifth see that the secondary valve works freely, and seats perfectly. Sixth see that the pneumatic and its connections are all right.

Tracing Leaks

In tracing out leaks, cover the tracker-board with a strip of sheep-skin as this material will prevent air from sucking in through the air ducts, better than paper.

Tester, How Used

When testing the player with the test roll, the tempo lever should be at Allegretto on a heavy pressure, and at Largo for a light pressure. Every note should speak with equal promptness; if not, the air duct is partially choked, or the primary or secondary valves are not properly regulated, or there is a leak caused by loose screws, or some portion of the wood work is split.

Power Pneumatics

The pneumatics being placed in a vacuum chest the air rushes into the pneumatic, and the vacuum on the inside moving it to operate the key, all its capacity of work has been absorbed by the pneumatics.

Spring

4. If this spring is too stiff it will accelerate, and if too weak it will slow the tempo.

The Orchestrelle

With this instrument it is possible to reproduce satisfactorily orchestral music. This instrument is excelled only by the great pipe-organ: it can be played with the key board, also with rolls of perforated paper, leaving the performer to control the stops and pedals only.

The Mechanism of the Vocalion or Orchestrelle

The tone in this instrument is produced by free reeds, and each reed is provided with a pipe or qualifying tube or an acoustic cell, one of various forms and dimensions, through which the tone passes this tube or pipe, and which determines the quality and character of tone and exercises a great influence on the sound produced by the vibrating tongue. It is this addition that gives the reed its fluty quality, as well as the resonance and power of tone. The toe of the tube or pipe rests in a hole that leads into the reed cell: by this means the tone of this instrument does not resemble that of the reed organ. Temperature has little effect on organs built on this plan, therefore they are usually in good tune. A change in temperature of from 15 to 20 degrees F. will change the pitch of the pipe organ a half tone. These organs only require about one-third the space of that of the pipe organ of equal capacity. The construction of the action is simple and it does not easily get out of order, and the reeds are easy of access. The construction of the bellows is on the force principle: this system has the advantage over the exhaust, as it forces the air through the reeds instead of sucking; thus preventing silent reeds caused by small particles of dust lodging between the tongue and the frame of the reed. The tone is thrown out rather than drawn into the organ, as in old style reed organs.

Tuning the Vocalion or Orchestrelle

The reeds are tuned the same as in the reed organ; except in some cases if only slightly out of tune, and the tube is furnished with a tuning coil or shade, they can be tuned by the coil or shade.

Vocalion or Orchestrelle Mechanism
(See Figure 21, page 205.)

1. Bellows: its use is to furnish organ with compressed wind. 2. Feeder: its use is to supply bellows. 3. Wind-chest or reservoir: its use is to distribute wind to the various wind chests. 4. Key valve: its use is to allow wind to enter the primary diaphragm chest 7. 5. Tracker-board: over it the perforated music sheet passes when the organ is used with self playing device. 6. Wind-chest. This chest is filled with compressed wind when the organ is played with a perforated music sheet. A stop admits or excludes wind to this chest as desired. 7. Primary diaphragm wind-chest. The compressed air in this chest operates the puppet valve 8. 8. Primary valve. When chest 7 is filled with wind the air lifts the diaphragm at the top of the chest on which rests a disk. To this disk is attached the spindle of the puppet valve 8. This upward motion caused by the diaphragm raises the puppet valve and closes the opening at the bottom of the chest 9, and opens it at the top of chest 10. The opening thus caused allows the compressed air in chest 10 to rush down into chest 9 and make its way through channel 22 to the secondary diaphragm chest 11. 9. Wind-chest: its use is to admit external and compressed wind to

chest 11. 10. Wind-chest. This chest is continually filled with compressed air. 11. Secondary diaphragm chest. When compressed wind is admitted to this chest, as above stated, it lifts the diaphragm at the top of the chest on which rests a disk.

12. Secondary valve. When compressed air is admitted to chest 11, it lifts the disk to which is attached the spindle of the secondary valve. This motion of the spindle opens the valve at the bottom and closes it at the top of chests 13 and 14, thus allowing the compressed air in chest 13, to rush down through opening thus made, which in turn allows the air to escape from chest 16 through channel 15.

13. Secondary wind chest. When the key is at rest and the duct in the tracker board is closed, this chest is filled with compressed air; and this wind pressure passing through channel 15 to chamber 16 inflates the diaphragm.

14. Wind chest. The air in this chest is continually under pressure. Its use is to fill chest 13 when valve 12 is closed.

15. Channel. This conveyance conducts external and compressed air by turns to chamber 16, thus allowing the diaphragm to collapse and inflate as the key is lowered and released.

16. Diaphragm chamber. Between this chamber and 17 is placed the diaphragm to which is attached a piece of cord to operate valve 18.

Fig. 21

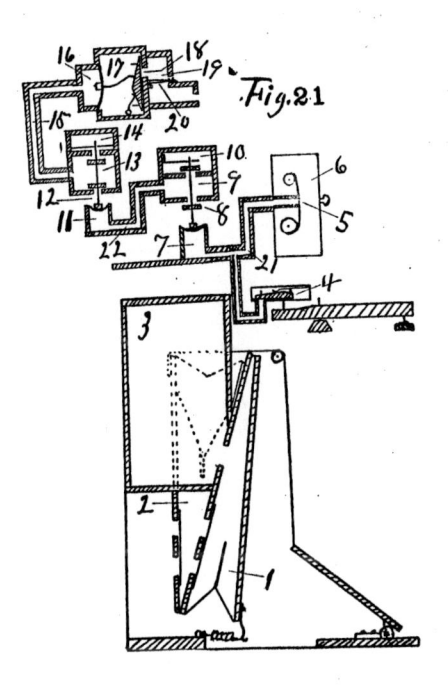

17. Reed valve chest. This is filled with compressed air.

18. Reed valve. Its use is to admit to and exclude air from chamber 19.

19. Reed cell.

20. Reed. When air is admitted to cell 19, it forces the tongue on reed 20 down, which immediately springs back again. This motion of the tongue sets the air in vibration and a tone is produced.

21-22. Wind channels.

CLASSIFICATION OF STOPS

This addenda is inserted for the convenience of the elementary student, whom it is hoped it may aid in deciphering the following classified list of stops.

This classification of stops is one commonly employed by voicers of organ pipes. It is intended to aid only the tuner in judging the different tone character of stops, and does not necessarily conform to the registration of some organists.

DIAPASON FAMILY.

Cymbel (mixture). The quality of tone is very bright and acute.

Contra. An octave below.

Cornet. A stop consisting of several ranks of pipes.

Double Open Diapason, 32 feet. The tone is large and powerful.

Diapason, 8 feet. The chief foundation stop of the organ. The tone is full and strong.

Dulciana Cornet. A stop consisting of several ranks of pipes. The tone is delicate.

Furniture. A compound stop from 2 to 5 ranks of pipes.

Grand Principal, 8 feet. The tone resembles that of the Diapason.

Gross Nazard, 5 1-3 feet. Sounding the fifth.

Horn Diapason, 8 feet, (wood).

Mixture. A mutation or compound-stop consisting of 2 to 7 ranks of pipes.

Nacht Horn, 8 feet. The tone resembles that of the Quintadena. It is of larger scale and more horn-like.

Nasard or Twelfth, 2 2-3 feet.

Octave, 4 feet.

Open Diapason, Major, 8 feet. Large scale.
" " *Minor,* 8 feet. Small scale.
" " 8 feet.

Octave Quint, 2 2-3 feet. Speaking the fifth.
Principal, 16-8 or 4 feet.
Prestant, 16 feet. Open Diapason.
Super Octave, 2 feet.
Sesquialtera, 2 2-3 feet, (Mixture).
Scharf, 1 1-3 feet. A shrill mixture stop.
Stentorphone, 8 feet. A very powerful tone.
Tuba Sonora, 8 feet. Tone very powerful. On a wind pressure of 22 inches.
Unda Maris, 8 feet, (Wave of the Sea). This stop consists of two sets of open metal pipes of small scale and delicate tone. One set being tuned a trifle sharper than the other, produces a waving, undulating effect, which is very beautiful.
Violin Diapason, 8 feet.

PEDAL ORGAN.

Grand Bourdon, 32 feet.
Gravissima (Resultant), 64 feet.
Gross Quint, Stopped, 10 2-3 feet. Sounding the fifth.
Gross Principal, 32 feet. Double Open Diapason.
Sub Bourdon, 32 feet. Double Stopped Diapason.
Sub Bass, 32 feet.
Sub Principal, 32 feet.

FLUTE FAMILY.

Concert Flute, 8 feet. The tone is full and gentle.
Clarabella, 8 feet. With powerful fluty tone.
Doppel Floete, 8 feet. The pipes are furnished with two mouths.
Flute Traverso, 8 feet. German Flute.
Flute Dolce, 8 feet. Of delicate intonation.
Flageolet, 2 feet. The tone is smaller than that of the Piccolo.
Flute D' Amour, 4 feet. Of delicate tone.
Flute Harmonic, 8 or 4 feet. The pipes are of double length, 8 or 16 feet. The bodies of the pipes have a hole bored in them midway between the top and the mouth. The tone is full and fluty.
Flute a Pavillon, 8 feet. The pipes of which are surmounted by a bell.
Flautino, 2 feet.

Gedäckt, 8 feet. Stopped pipe.
Gross Flute, 8 feet. Very powerful and strong tone.
Hohl Flute, 8 feet. Hollow-toned Flute. The tone is thick and powerful. This pipe has two holes in it near the top, opposite each other.
Hohlpfeife, 4 feet. The pipe has two mouths and the tone is very bright.
Lieblich Gedäckt, 8 feet. A stopped pipe of slender scale. The tone is subdued and of remarkable beauty.
Melodia, 8 feet. Tone mellow.
Piccolo, 2 feet. The tone is bright and clear.
Rohrflöte, 8 feet. A stop of gentle intonation and slightly reedy.
Spitz Flute, 8 feet. The tone is soft and pleasing, the pipes are conical in shape.
Stopped Diapason, 8 feet.
Wald Flute, 4 feet. The tone is of medium power. (Forest-flute).

STRING FAMILY.

Aeoline, 8 feet. The softest stop used.
Contra-Gamba, 16 feet. A stop representing the Violoncello.
Dulciana, 8 or 16 feet. Tone soft and sweet.
Dolce, 8 feet. Of delicate intonation.
Dulcissimo, 8 feet. A soft and delicate tone.
Dulcet, 4 feet. Tone soft and sweet.
Cornet. 5 rank mixture of Dulciana scale.
Fugara, 4 feet. Resembling the Gamba in tone.
Grossgambe, 8 feet. Tone full or grand.
Gamba, 8 feet. Its tone is pungent and somewhat like the violin or violoncello.
Gemshorn, 8, 4 or 2 feet. The tone is light and clear, the pipes are conical and tuned with the ears.
Geigen Principal, 8 feet. The tone is crisp, (Violin Diapason).
Gambette, 4 feet. Small or octave Gamba.
Keraulophon, 8 feet. The tone is soft and pleasing, it seldom extends below small c. This peculiar

tone is obtained by boring a small hole in the body of the pipe near the top.

Quintadena, 8 feet.

Quintaton, 16 feet. Of smaller scale than the Diapason, sounding the twelfth as well as the fundamental tone.

Salicional, 8 feet. The tone is of medium power.

Viola, 8 feet. Tone of medium power, and similar to the Violin.

Violin, 4 feet. The tone is gentle.

Viola D' Amour, 8 feet. Quality of tone similar to the Gamba.

Violoncello, 8 feet. Small scale with crisp tone.

Vox Celestis, 8 feet. A stop tuned sharper than the others (2 ranks).

Viol D' Orchestre, 8 feet. The tone is very pungent and stringy.

REED FAMILY.

Euphone, 16 feet. Free reed, smooth tone.

Fagotto, 8 feet. Very small scale trumpet.

Contra Fagotto, 16 feet. An octave lower than the fagotto.

Horn, 8 feet. A smooth toned trumpet.

Hautbois, Oboe, Hautboy, 8 feet. Imitation of the orchestral instrument.

Harmonic Trumpet,
" *Clarion,* Having pipes double length, to improve the quality and quantity of tone. Usually in the treble.

Musette, 4 feet. A reed stop of soft intonation.

Orchestral Trumpet,
" *Clarinet,*
" *Oboe,* 8 feet. Voiced more brilliant, in imitation of the instrument. Distinctive of the subdued voicing for church purposes.

Ophicleide, 16 feet. Large scale trumpet.

Phisarmonica, 16 feet. A free reed.

Posaune, 16 feet. Trumpet, medium or small scale.

Saxophone, 4 feet. Soft tone, imitation of instrument.

Trombone, 16 feet. Large scale trumpet. Usually a pedal stop.
Tromba, 8 feet. Trumpet. Usually a pedal stop.
Tuba, 8 feet. A large scale solo trumpet, voiced on very heavy wind-pressure.
Vox Humana, 8 feet. To resemble the human voice.
Vox Angelica, 8 feet. A free reed, soft and smooth.
Bombarde, 16 feet. Large scale trumpet. Voiced more robust than the ophicleide.
Bassoon, 8 feet. The bass of oboe.
Contra Bombarde, 32 feet. An octave lower than bombarde.
Contra Fagotto, 32 feet. An octave lower than fagotto, etc.
Clarion, 4 feet. Trumpet (any scale).
Cor-Anglaise, 8 feet. English horn (Cornopean).
Clarinet, 8 feet. Imitation of instrument.
Cornopean, 8 feet. Trumpet. Large scale trumpet; voiced smooth and full (Swell organ trumpet).

Diaphon, 16 feet Reed Pipe. Tone produced by a vibrating valve, instead of a tongue of brass.
Echo Vox Humana, 8 feet. In the echo organ.
Echo Trumpet, 8 feet. In the echo organ.

INDEX
R. O.—REED ORGAN.

A

Action, Detailed, of the tracker organ 42
"   Electric 109, 117
"   Electro pneumatic 109, 111
"   of the key movement 35
"   " tracker organ 42, 44
"   pneumatic 94
"   R. O. 145
"   Tubular 95
"   "   pneumatic inflate 96, 99, 102
"   "   "   stop 96
Addition of pedals 12
"   " reed pipes 14
Advantages of electric action 109
Aeolian interior player 184
"   piano; How tuned 184
Ancient organs with two key boards 13
Anemometer...................................89
Angelus: How to take it apart 196
"   interior player mechanism: How to take it apart 197
"   player 188
"   To tune the piano to 192
Arrangement of the pipes 32
"   "   " ribs 22
Armature 122
Automatic valve to prevent ciphering R. O. 144

B

Back-fall frame 33
Balancing of stops 121
Beard of Pipe 47
Bearers 30
Bellows and its use 17
"   bottom-board 23
"   Concussion 26, 89

Bellows	Defects in	72
"	Description of	23
"	effects speech of pipe	73
"	Figure 4	16
"	handle	25
"	How they were fastened	8
"	middle board	18
"	" and bottom board valves	19
"	" board panels	19
"	runs down too soon	73
"	repairing	25
"	Weight of	19

Blowing action 22
" of the organ 21
Body in unison with tongue 58
Borrowed stops 120
Breathy tone 80
Bung 28

C

Cause of clattering sound 73
" " gasping sound 73
" " low dull sound 69
" " moaning sound 72
" " robbing 74
Celeste reeds R. O. 141
Channel board: How to take off 182
Character of reed tone 58
" " tone influenced by dimensions 49
" " tone R. O. 141
Choir Organ 149
Ciphering caused by key movement 68
" keys 103, 118
" reasons for 67
" reed organ 130
" prevented by automatic valve R. O. ...144
Classification of stops 207
Clattering sound, Cause of 73
Cleaning reed organ 137
" " tongue R. O. 137
Closed work 63
Compass of key board 11

Compass of pipes 60
Compensating organ 168
Complete and incomplete stops 120
Compound stops 64
Concussion bellows 26, 89
Console, Movable 117
" Plan of 124
Construction of large organ 10
" " reed organ 124
Contacts, Electric 116
Counter-balance 24
Coupler 38-39
" action, Electric 115
" pedal 39
" ram 71
Curving of tongue 88
Cutting down new pipes 85

D

Defects in key movement 70
" " the bellows 72
Dented pipes: How remedied 76
Detailed action of the tracker organ 42
Description of bellows 23
" " tone 64
Destruction of organs 14
Diapason stop taken as a standard 64
" work 63
Dip of Key 41
Direction pins 29
Draw-stop action 39

E

Earliest use of semitones 12
Early construction of large organs 10
" types of players 168
Ears of pipes 47
Echo organ 152
Effect of moisture and heat on the player ..188
Electric action 109, 111, 117
" " coupler 115
" " contacts 116
" " Repetition of 117
" stop action 118

Electro pneumatic action 109, 111
Enemies of the pipe organ 82
Escape-valve 25
Exhaust R. O. 126
Explanation of figure 18 192
" " motor governor 193
Extreme length of organ pipes 60

F

Fan-frame movement 33
Faults, How to remedy in wind chest of reed
      organ 130
" of player 199
Feeders 19
" Repairing 25
Feeder, Square 22
Figure 1 Wind chest 7
" 2 Bellows 7
" 3 Hydraulic organ 7
" 4 Bellows and pipes 16
" 5 Concussion bellows and wind gauge ..20
" 6 Tracker organ 34
" 7 Pneumatic action and ram coupler ...37
" 8 Pneumatic lever 93
" 9 " action 97
" 10 Tubular pneumatic action 100
" 11 Electric action 110
" 12 " " 112
" 13 " coupler action 114
" 14 Piano player 170
" 15 " " 174
" 16 Simplex player 177
" 17 Pianola 183
" 18 The Angelus player 189
" 18 The explanation of 192
" 19 Motor governor, Angelus 194
" 20 Reed organ 125
" 21 Vocalion or Orchestrelle 205
" 22 Tubular pneumatic action 105
" 23 " " " 106
Fingers or key levers: How fastened 191
First organ building in America................17
" use of the wind chest 5

Flue pipe, Pitch of 59
" pipes: How tuned 84
Folds or ribs 23
Free reeds 57
Front-board or bung 28

G

Gasping sound, Cause of 73
Grand Concert Organ..........................147

H

How reeds are tuned R. O. 135
" the key levers or fingers are fastened....191
"   " player is operated 172
"   " tone is produced R .O. 134
"   to change pitch R. O. 139
"   " determine pitch of reeds R. O. 135
"   " raise the languid 80
"   " remove piano action 197
"   " take off channel board 182
"   "   " out Angelus interior player mechanism 197
"   "   "   " pneumatic action 198
"   "   "   " the player action 187
"   "   "   "   " pneumatic-chest 185
"   "   "   "   " reeds 196
"   "   " the Angelus apart 196
"   "   "   " Pianola apart 181
"   " test pitch R. O. 136
"   "   " the organ 123
"   " use the Tester.......................201
"   tongues are filed 137
Humming caused by slider 69
Hydraulic or water-organ 8

I

Improved key board 13
Individual wind-chests 119
Inflate tubular pneumatic action 96, 98, 99, 104
Influence of stops 121
Intonation of pipes 58
Inventor of bellows 18
Inverted ribs 19

J

K

Key board, Compass of 11
Key board, Improved 13
Key levers or fingers: How fastened 191
Key movement 35
" " Defects of 70
Keys 32
" cipher 103, 118
" Leveling R. O. 146
" Stick R. O. 145
Kinds of reeds 57

L

Languid: How to raise 80
" Position of 80
Largest manual stop 64
Leakage 74
" R. O. 127
Leaks, Tracing 200
Length of pipes with reference to harmonic
 series 66
Length of stopped pipes 48
Leveling keys 71
" " R. O. 146
Low dull sound, Cause of 69
Lubricating parts 200
Lug 23

M

Mechanism of the vocalion or orchestrelle ...201
Metal, Poor: How detected 45
" Preparation of 46
Middle board 18
" " panels 19
" and bottom board valves 19
" frame 21, 24
Mixture stops where the break occurs 122
Mixtures: How tuned 88
Moaning sound, Cause of 72
Modern pneumatic or wind organ 17

Motor 123
" governor, Explanation of 193
" Pneumatic 169
" Spring 169
" will not run 187
Mouth of wooden pipe 55
Movable console 117
Music sheet does not track properly 197
Mutation stops 63
Mutes, Position of R. O. 142

N

New strings put in and squeaking pedals fixed ..184
New tongues R. O. 136
Noisy spring motor 186

O

Octaves, To couple 115
Orchestrelle 201
" or vocalion mechanism 203
" " " Mechanism of 201
" " " To tune 202
Organ building in America 17
" How cleaned R. O. 137
" How to test 123
" How tuned R. O. 139
" Pitch of 81
Organs with two key boards 13
Overblowing or speaking the octave 79

P

Pallet: How covered 67
Pallets 29, 119
Panel 24
Parts of piano-player 169
" " reed organ 124
" " " pipes 56
" " the Pianola 182
Pedal couplers 39
" organ 152
" reeds R. O., Position of 133
" straps: How to put in R. O. 146
" " R. O. 145
" Addition of 12

Piano action: How removed 197
" player 168
Pianola: How to take it apart 181
" Parts of 182
" player 181
Pipe badly dented: How remedied 76
" Mouth of wooden 55
" racks 30
" speaking its octave 77
Pipes, Arrangement of 32
" changed by atmospheric causes 77
" Compass of 60
" effected by the bellows 73
" Extreme length of 60
" furnished with ears and beard 47
" How they vibrate 52
" How to change the speech of 77
" " " cut down 85
" " tuned 84, 86
" Length of stopped 48
" Most common faults of speech of 78
" of various shapes 46
" overblowing or speaking their octaves ..79
" Parts of wooden 47
" Pitch of flue 53
" rattle, Reed 91
" Reed, placed on a heavier wind 55
" refuse to speak 81
" Scale of 62
" Silent reed 92
" Sounds how produced in 47
" speaking their octave or fifth 54
" Spotted metal 45
" tremble caused by wind 76
" with trembling tone 75
" " weak waving tone 75
Pitch, changed according to stops used 60
" " R. O. 139
" How changed 83
" " to test R. O. 136
" of flue pipes 59
" " organs 81
" " pipe 53

Pitch of reed pipes 59
Plan of console 124
Player action: How to take out 187
" Aeolian interior 184
" Faults of 199
" How affected by moisture and heat 188
" " cleaned 180
" " operated 172
" Pianola 181
" Simplex 176, 185
" The Angelus 188
Players, Self 119
Pneumatic action: How taken out 198
" " Tubular 94
" acts when it should not: Reasons
why 179
" chest: How to take out 185
" does not act 200
" inflate action 104
" key action 95
" lever 92
" motor 169
" or wind organ 17
" piano player action 173
" will not act: Reasons why 178
Pneumatics, Power 201
" Principle of 92
Poor metal: How detected 45
Position of lips and languid 80
" " pedal reeds R. O. 133
Positive organ 13
Power pneumatics 201
Preparation of metal 46
Pressure of wind 25
Primary and secondary valves 199
Principle of pneumatics ,.....................92
Prompt speech of organ 27
Pull-down wire 28
Pump-rod 23

Q

Qualifying tubes R. O. 142
Quality of tone: How produced 78

R

Racks 30
Ram coupler 71
Rattling reeds R. O. 138
Reasons for organ's ciphering 67
   "   why pneumatics will not act 178
   "   " the pneumatic acts when it should
              not 179
Reed covered with leather 90
  " organ action 145
  "   "   Construction of 124
  "   "   exhaust 126
  "   "   How tuned 139
  "   "   leakage 127
  "   "   Parts of 124
  "   "   pitch: How changed 139
  "   "   wind-chest 129
  " pipes, Addition of 14
  "   "   Parts of 56
  "   "   Pitch of 59
  "   "   placed on a heavier wind 55
  "   "   rattle 91
  "   "   silent 92
  " scraper R. O. 147
  " tone, Character of 58
  " voicing block 89
  "   " R. O. 139
Reeds, Celeste R. O. 141
  " Ciphering R. O. 130
  " Free 57
  " get out of order R. O. 136
  " How to determine the pitch of 135
  "   " tuned 135
  " Kinds of 57
  " of Angelus: How to take out 196
  " Rattling R. O. 138
  " Silent R. O. 142
  " Size of R. O. 136
  " sounding the semitone above and below 133
  " Speaking, and stops R. O. 143
  " striking 57
  " Study of R. O. 133
  " Vibration of 58

Remedies of faults in wind chest of R. O. 130
Repetition of electric action 117
Resonance R. O. 142
Result of closed swell 83
Ribs, Arrangement of 22, 24
" Inverted 19
Robbing, Cause of 74
" How tested 74
Rollers 36
Running of air ....,....29, 68

S

Scale of organ pipes 62
Scraping noise: How remedied ....,.....79
Secondary and primary valves 199
Self players 119
Semitones, Earliest use of 12
Silent reeds R. O. 142
Simplex player 176, 185
Size of reeds R. O. 136
Slider causing humming 69
Sliders 30
Solo organ 151
Sound: How produced 47
Sounding-board 27, 28, 35
Sound-producing portion of the organ 44
Specifications of grand concert organ 157
Speech of organ 27
"   "   pipe affected by bellows 73
Spotted metal pipes 45
Spring 201
"   motor 169
"   "   noisy 186
Square feeder 22
Squares 38
Squeaking pedals fixed and new strings put in 184
Stop action, Electric 118
"   "   Pneumatic 96
"   draws too far 40
"   "   "   hard 40
"   R. O. 145

Stops and speaking reeds R. O. 143
" Balancing of 121
" Borrowed 120
" Classification of 207
" Complete and incomplete 120
" Compound 64
" Description of tone and name of 64
" Influence of 121
" Largest manual 64
" Mixture, where the break occurs 122
" Mutation 63
" taken for standard 64
Straps, Pedal, R. O. 145
"   "   How to put in 146
Striking reeds 57
Study of reeds R. O. 133
Swell closed, Result of 83
Swell organ 150

T

Table giving names of octaves 60
"   of vibrations of flue and reed pipes 59
Temperament 82
Temperature at which to tune 81
Tester: How used 201
Thumping-board 32
To clean the player 180
" couple octaves 115
" fix squeaking pedals and put in new strings 184
Tone character influenced by dimensions 49
"   "   R. O. 141
" how produced R. O. 134
" influenced by thick metal or wood 55
" of reeds and position of mutes R. O. 142
" quality: How produced 78
" resonance R. O. 142
" trembling 75
" uneven 75
Tongue, Curving of reed 88
"   How fastened 56
"   "   'it vibrates 56

Tongues damaged by kinks 87
"   How cleaned R. O. 137
"   "   filed R. O. 137
"   New R. O. 136
Top-board 24
Tracing leaks 200
Tracker action 42, 44
"   organ 27
"   "   wind chest 119
Trackers 33
Trembling tone 75
Tremolo 41
"   R. O. 144
Trunk-band 23
Tubes, Qualifying 142
Tubular pneumatic action 94, 102
"   "   inflate action 96, 98, 99
"   "   key action 95
"   "   stop action 96
Tuning mixtures 88
"   reed organ 139
"   the Aeolian piano 184
"   "   piano to the Angelus 192
"   "   Vocalion or Orchestrelle 202

U

Uneven tone 75

V

Valve-holes 23
Valves 29
"   and how they were connected 6
"   Middle and bottom board 19
Various shapes of pipes 46
Vibration of pipe 52
"   "   reed tongues 58
"   "   tongues 56
Vibrations, Table of 59
Vocalion or Orchestrelle mechanism 203
"   "   "   Mechanism of 201
"   "   "   To tune 202
Voicing 50, 89
"   reeds R. O. 139

W

Water-organ 8
Waver in tone, Cause of 75
Weight, Bellows 19, 25
Wholesale destruction of organs 14
Why reeds get out of order R. O. 136
Wind box 21
" causing pipes to tremble 76
" chest 27
" " First use of 5
" " ·Individual 119
" " reed organ 129
" " tracker organ 119
" gauge 19
" pressure 25
" trunks 26
" way too deep 54
Windy or breathy tone 80
Wooden pipes, Parts of 47
" " that are tuned by a shade 86

BOSTON

MB

Copyright © 2006 Merchant Books

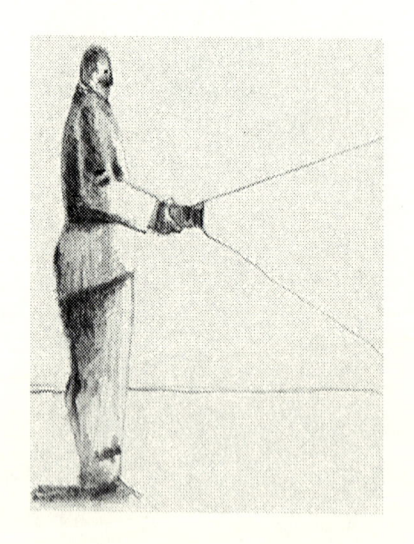

Printed in the United States
59995LVS00003B/5